"Practical, useful information and techniques for putting the body's natural abilities to work on healing—a wonderful contribution."

—Dr. Wayne Dyer
author of *There's a Spiritual Solution to Every Problem*

"Dr. Sha is an important teacher and a wonderful healer with a valuable message about the power of the soul to influence and transform all life."

—Dr. Masaru Emoto
author of *The Hidden Messages in Water*

"Dr. Sha makes available secret techniques and insights that were available in the past only to a select few. He shares in simple terms the insights and tools that took him more than thirty years of hard work and discipline to attain. He gives you access to information that would otherwise be unattainable."

—Dr. John Gray
author of *Men Are from Mars, Women Are from Venus*

"We, the human race, need more Zhi Gang Sha."

—Dr. Maya Angelou
author of *I Know Why the Caged Bird Sings*

"Dr. Sha offers a clear, practical path to learning the secrets of self-healing."

—Marianne Williamson
author of *A Return to Love*

"The Tao Song that Master Sha sings is a musical gift. There is a purity and a resonance that only he can lay claim to. His voice is like the voice of God singing."

—Roberta Flack
Grammy Award–winning musician

TAO CALLIGRAPHY HEALING FIELD

TAO CALLIGRAPHY HEALING FIELD

AN INFORMATION SYSTEM WITH SIX SACRED TAO TECHNIQUES TO EMPOWER YOU TO HEAL AND TRANSFORM YOUR LIFE

DR. & MASTER ZHI GANG SHA

The information contained in this book is intended to be educational and not for diagnosis, prescription, or treatment of any health disorder whatsoever. The content of this book is intended to be used as an adjunct to a rational and responsible healthcare program prescribed by a healthcare practitioner. The author and publisher are in no way liable for any misuse of the material.

Published by Heaven's Library Publication Corp.
and Waterside Productions

Heaven's Library Waterside Productions

Heaven's Library Publication Corp.
30 Wertheim Court, Unit 27D
Richmond Hill, ON L4B 1B9 Canada
www.heavenslibrary.com
heavenslibrary@drsha.com

Waterside Productions
2055 Oxford Ave.
Cardiff, CA 92007
www.waterside.com

ISBN: 978-1-949003-16-1 print-on-demand
ISBN: 978-1-949003-17-8 e-book
ISBN: 978-1-949003-15-4 hardcover

Design: Lynda Chaplin
Illustrations: Henderson Ong
Animations: Hardeep Kharbanda
Audio: Zhi Gang Sha

Contents

List of Figures

How to Do the Practices in This Book

THIS BOOK INCLUDES WISDOM, knowledge, and many practices for healing and transforming your health, relationships, finances, and more. In fact, all of my books are a blend of teaching and practice. Practice is essential for healing and transformation. Wisdom without practice is only theory. Practice without wisdom could be incorrect.

This book includes more than twenty sacred practices and powerful mantras taught to me by Tao Source. For you, dear reader, I am delighted to include with this book animated videos to support you in your practice. In each one, you will be guided clearly step by step to do the most important practices in this book. I also chant the sacred mantras for each practice, so that you can actually do each practice together with the animations and my chanting.

Practice. Practice. Practice.

Experience the healing.

Experience the transformation.

With love and blessing,

Dr. and Master Zhi Gang Sha

Access the practice videos

Use the URL below or scan the QR code with your smartphone or other appropriate device to access the videos. A special app is not required.

https://tchf.heavenslibrary.com

How to scan a QR code with your Android device

1. Launch the camera on your device.
2. Point it at the QR code.
3. Follow the instructions that appear on your screen.

How to scan a QR code with your iOS device

1. Launch the camera on your device.
2. Hold your device so that the QR code appears in the camera's viewfinder. Your device recognizes the QR code and shows a notification.
3. Tap the notification to open the link associated with the QR code.

Introduction

HUMANITY AND MOTHER EARTH are in a special time. Many people have great challenges in health, relationships, or finances. Many severe natural disasters are occurring. Political and economic challenges exist throughout the world. Humanity is facing challenges in the soul, heart, mind, and body.

Millions of people are searching for solutions to their challenges. They use conventional medicine, traditional Chinese medicine, complementary and alternative medicine, yoga, Reiki, qigong, tai chi, and more. They follow teachings of mindfulness, meditation, and all kinds of spiritual paths. These teachings and practices are supported by a body of research on the benefits of energy (qi) cultivation, mindfulness, meditation, gratitude, forgiveness, and more. Millions of people are truly searching for healing and transformation.

Surveys and studies show that people invest a great deal of resources—financial, time, energy—as they seek health, wellness, prevention of sickness, self-healing, a healthy lifestyle, and more. See figure 1, which breaks down global spending on health and wellness in 2017.

People want inner peace and inner joy in their health, relationships, finances, and more. How can we help humanity overcome all kinds of challenges and achieve inner peace and inner joy? How can you gain inner peace and inner joy?

Source: Global Wellness Institute, Global Wellness Economy Monitor, October 2018

Figure 1. Global wellness economy

At this special time, I feel that love, peace, and harmony are very much needed by you, your family, community, city, and country, and Mother Earth.

Why are people unhealthy? Why do people have relationship challenges? Why do people have financial challenges? In one sentence:

Challenges in health, relationships, and finances are due to health, relationships, and finances not being in love, peace, and harmony.

How can we bring love, peace, and harmony to you, humanity, and Mother Earth? We can start with meditation.

Meditation can bring inner peace and inner joy. Hundreds of styles of meditation have been developed over thousands of years. Many meditation techniques are very powerful; they can transform one's health, relationships, or finances.

In this book, I am honored to integrate ancient and modern sacred wisdom and practical techniques to heal and transform your health, relationships, finances, and more. The wisdom and techniques are simple and powerful. They could quickly benefit your health, relationships, and finances.

Challenges in health, relationships, finances, and every aspect of life carry blocked energies. The blockages create a negative field. To heal and transform the challenges is to transform the negative field to a positive field.

This book shares six sacred Tao power techniques—six sacred techniques from Tao Source to create a positive field for love, peace, and harmony in health, relationships, finances, and every aspect of life.

Ancient wisdom revealed a sacred universal law, the Law of Shen Qi Jing. Shen 神 includes *soul, heart, and mind*. Qi 氣 means *energy*. Jing 精 means *matter*. The Law of Shen Qi Jing states that everyone and everything is made of shen, qi, and jing and explains the immutable relationships among shen, qi, and jing. (For simplicity, I will henceforth use "shen qi jing" to mean *shen, qi, and jing*.)

Einstein's famous formula, $E = mc^2$, expresses the physical law that mass and energy are equivalent. It states that the equivalent energy (E) can be calculated as the mass (m) multiplied by the square of the speed of light (c).

Dr. Rulin Xiu and I co-created Tao Science,[1] a science of creation and grand unification that unifies scientific and spiritual wisdom. We shared

[1] See *Tao Science: The Science, Wisdom, and Practice of Creation and Grand Unification* by Dr. Rulin Xiu and me (Cardiff, CA/Richmond Hill, ON: Waterside Press, Heaven's Library Publication Corp., 2017).

with humanity the grand unification formula, S + E + M = 1. In this formula, S denotes *shen*, E *energy*, and M *matter*. "1" signifies the *Tao Source Oneness Field*, which is the grand unified field.

Tao is the Source. The Source is Tao. Tao Science explains that all sickness and all challenges and blockages in health, relationships, finances, and every aspect of life are due to shen qi jing not being aligned as one (S + E + M ≠ 1).

A human being is made of shen qi jing. An animal is made of shen qi jing. An ocean is made of shen qi jing. A mountain is made of shen qi jing. Cities and countries are made of shen qi jing. Mother Earth is made of shen qi jing. Mother Earth is one planet. There are countless planets, stars, galaxies, and universes. They are all made of shen qi jing.

The Law of Shen Qi Jing further states:

靈到心到	ling dao xin dao	Soul arrives, heart follows.
心到意到	xin dao yi dao	Heart arrives, mind follows.
意到氣到	yi dao qi dao	Mind arrives, energy follows.
氣到血到	qi dao xue dao	Energy arrives, matter follows.

ling dao xin dao

"Ling 靈" means *soul*. Both quantum science and Tao Science teach about information or message. In my opinion, information in the scientific field and soul or spirit in the spiritual realm are the same thing.

"Dao 到" means *to arrive*. "Xin 心" means *heart*. "Ling dao xin dao" means *soul or information arrives, heart arrives*. This tells us that the soul is the boss. The soul leads the heart. This heart is more than the physical heart. It is the emotional and spiritual heart in everyone and everything. This heart is the receiver of the information or message. If one's heart is only ten percent open, one will receive ten percent of the message, including ten percent of its benefits. If one's heart is fully open, one will receive full benefits of the message. Therefore, opening the heart is sacred wisdom and practice for healing and transforming every aspect of life.

xin dao yi dao

"Yi 意" means *consciousness,* which includes superficial consciousness, deep consciousness, subconsciousness, minimal consciousness, perceptual consciousness, access consciousness, phenomenal consciousness, and more. Since ancient times they have all been expressed as "yi." Yi can also mean *thought.* In modern times, we connect consciousness and thought—the mind—with the brain (nao 腦). "Xin dao yi dao" literally means *heart arrives, mind arrives* or *heart arrives, mind follows.* In other words, *the heart passes the information or message to the mind.* The mind is the processor of the message.

yi dao qi dao

"Qi 氣" means *energy.* "Yi dao qi dao" means *the mind passes the message to the energy.* Energy is the mover.

qi dao xue dao

"Xue 血" means *blood,* which represents matter. "Qi dao xue dao" means *the energy passes the message to the matter.* Matter is the transformer.

These four phrases in the Law of Shen Qi Jing—ling dao xin dao, xin dao yi dao, yi dao qi dao, qi dao xue dao—explain the relationships among shen qi jing. These relationships can be understood as follows:

- ling (soul, spirit, information): content of message
- xin (heart, core of life): receiver of message
- nao (brain, mind, consciousness): processor of message
- qi (energy): mover of message
- jing (matter): transformer of message

This is sacred wisdom and practice.

The soul sends the message or information to the heart, which delivers it to the mind, which in turn passes it to the energy, which finally sends it to the matter, resulting in an action, behavior, word, or thought. After the matter transforms the message in this way, the transformed message (action, behavior, word, or thought) is given as feedback to the soul. The soul will give a new message. This is the sacred process in one's whole being.

The Law of Shen Qi Jing explains the information system of a being. Like everything in the yin-yang world, this information system can be divided into yin and yang as the positive information system and the negative information system.

The sacred wisdom of this information system can explain:

- why people get sick
- why people have relationship and financial challenges
- why people have any kind of challenge in life

The one-sentence secret is:

All challenges in life are due to negative shen qi jing; all healthy conditions, inner peace, inner joy, and success are due to positive shen qi jing.

Therefore, this information system can also explain:

- how sickness can be healed
- how relationship and financial challenges can be transformed
- how any kind of challenge in life can be overcome

Healing and transformation for all life, including health, relationships, finances, and more, can be summarized in one sentence:

To heal and transform all life, transform negative shen qi jing to positive shen qi jing.

Frequency and vibration form a field. The frequency and vibration of positive shen qi jing form a positive field. The frequency and vibration of negative shen qi jing form a negative field.

Because shen qi jing form an information system, information is the key to transform all life. To transform all life is to create positive information. Then, positive heart, positive mind, positive energy, and positive matter will follow.

The six sacred Tao power techniques and wisdom that I present in this book create positive information. They work together to create a positive field. Applying any one of these six techniques is powerful. Applying all six sacred techniques together is beyond powerful. Applying the six sacred Tao power techniques together could bring heart-touching and heart-moving results to transform your health, relationships, and finances beyond comprehension.

This book is simple and very practical. Apply the wisdom and do the practices daily. Practice with the animations that you are given access to as part of this book and chant along with me. Practice for five to ten minutes a day and you could feel the frequency and vibration. Practice for one hour a day or more and you could receive remarkable benefits for your health, relationships, or finances.

An ancient teaching says, "If you want to know if a pear is sweet, taste it." If you want to know if these six sacred Tao power techniques and wisdom are powerful, experience them.

Tao Calligraphy Power and five other sacred power techniques (Body Power, Soul Power, Sound Power, Mind Power, Breath Power) create a positive field that can serve you with healing and transformation for all life.

Two decades ago, I gave this message of empowerment for healing to humanity:

I have the power to heal and transform myself.
You have the power to heal and transform yourself.
Together we have the power to heal and transform the world.

This book shares the sacred wisdom and techniques to achieve great healing and transformation.

This book can create a positive shen qi jing field from Tao Source to heal and transform all life.

This book can guide you to transform a negative shen qi jing field to a positive shen qi jing field in any aspect of life.

This book can help humanity and Mother Earth create a Love Peace Harmony World Family.

Practice. Practice. Practice.

Experience the healing.

Experience the transformation.

I love my heart and soul
I love all humanity
Join hearts and souls together
Love, peace, and harmony
Love, peace, and harmony

1

Tao Calligraphy

CALLIGRAPHY IS AN ART. Calligraphy has been a popular artistic and cultural form throughout history and around the world. There is hardly a country, a written language, or a people—contemporary or ancient—for whom calligraphy has not been significant. Among them are Chinese, peoples of other East Asian and Southeast Asian countries, Tibetans, Celts, Greeks, Persians, writers of Latin, Germans, Italians, Bengalis, and many more.

What is Tao Calligraphy?

Tao Calligraphy is based on Chinese calligraphy. There have been many styles of calligraphy in Chinese history. Tao Calligraphy is based on the style named Yi Bi Zi (一筆字), which means *one-stroke character*. I learned Yi Bi Zi from the late Professor Li Qiuyun, the sole lineage holder of Tai Shi (太師), the "supreme teacher" of the imperial court of the last emperor of China.

Yi Bi Zi is oneness writing. In Chinese, written characters are formed using sixteen basic types of strokes. These components of a Chinese character are somewhat analogous in function to the twenty-six letters in the English alphabet, although written Chinese is logosyllabic, unlike English.

The sixteen fundamental strokes are shown in figure 2 on the next page.

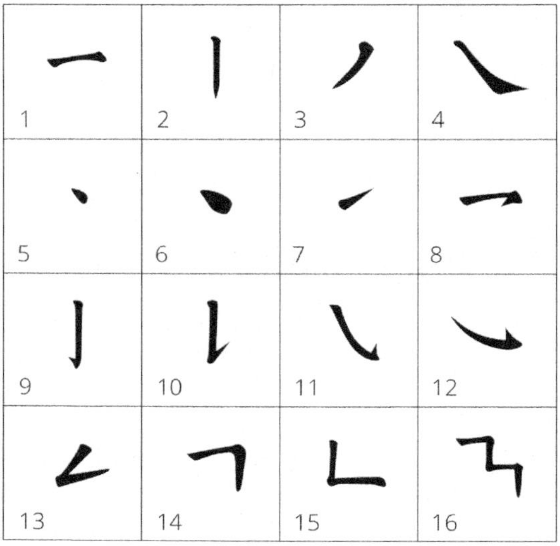

Figure 2. Sixteen basic strokes in Chinese characters

1. héng (横, horizontal, pronounced *hung*)
2. shù (豎, vertical, pronounced *shoo*)
3. piě (撇, downward and left, pronounced *pyeh*)
4. nà (捺, downward and right, pronounced *nah*)
5. xiǎo diǎn (小點, small dot, pronounced *shee-yow dyen*)
6. dà diǎn (大點, big dot, pronounced *dah dyen*)
7. tí (提, upward, pronounced *tee*)
8. héng gōu (横鉤, horizontal hook, pronounced *hung gō*)
9. shù gōu (豎鉤, vertical hook, pronounced *shoo gō*)
10. fǎn gōu (反鉤, vertical mirror hook, pronounced *fahn gō*)
11. xié gōu (斜鉤, slanted hook, pronounced *shyeh gō*)
12. wān gōu (彎鉤, curved hook, pronounced *wahn gō*)
13. zuǒ zhé (左折, left turn, pronounced *zwaw juh*)
14. yòu zhé (右折, right turn, pronounced *yō juh*)
15. xià zhé (下折, downward turn, pronounced *shyah juh*)
16. lián zhé (連折, multiple turns, pronounced *lyen juh*)

Let me explain Yi Bi Zi. The Chinese character "ai" (see figure 3) means *love*. In normal traditional Chinese writing,[2] this character is written with thirteen individual strokes. Yi Bi Zi unites these thirteen components as one continuous stroke. This is Oneness writing.

Figure 3. Chinese character "ai" (love): traditional script (left) and Yi Bi Zi (right)

---

[2] As opposed to simplified Chinese writing, which differs from traditional script for "ai" and for many other (but not all) characters.

When I write an Yi Bi Zi calligraphy, I connect with Tao Source and with sacred wisdom, practice, codes, saints, buddhas, and more. They pour Tao Source shen qi jing with the ten greatest qualities[3] of Tao Source into the calligraphy. The Yi Bi Zi calligraphy is transformed to Tao Calligraphy.

Power and significance of Tao Calligraphy

A powerful ancient wisdom is:

shu neng zai dao
書能載道

"Shu" means *calligraphy*. "Neng" means *to be able*. "Zai" means *to carry*. "Dao" is *Tao Source*. "Shu neng zai dao" means *calligraphy can carry Tao*.

Tao Calligraphy is Oneness writing. In *Dao De Jing*, Lao Zi wrote:

道生一	Dao sheng yi	Tao creates One
一生二	yi sheng er	One creates Two
二生三	er sheng san	Two creates Three
三生萬物	san sheng wan wu	Three creates wan wu (all things)

Tao is the Source. "One" signifies *hun dun yi qi*. "Hun dun" means *blurred*. "Yi" means *One*. "Qi" means *energy*. "Hun dun yi qi" denotes *the blurred Oneness condition*.

Tao is the ultimate Creator. Tao creates One, which is hun dun yi qi. Within the blurred Oneness condition there are two qi: 清氣 qing qi and 濁氣 zhuo qi. "Qing qi" means *clean* or *light qi*. "Zhuo qi" means *disturbed* or *heavy qi*. These two qi are mixed. They are not distinguished or separate. This is the blurred Oneness condition.

One creates Two. This blurred Oneness condition persists for eons. It waits for the time for qi transformation. When the qi transformation occurs, qing qi (clean qi) rises to form Heaven and zhuo qi (disturbed qi)

---

[3] I will explain these ten greatest natures of Tao Source in chapter two. They are the qualities of most positive shen qi jing.

falls to create Mother Earth. This is Lao Zi's wisdom on the creation of Heaven and Mother Earth.

Two creates Three. "Three" means *the blurred Oneness condition plus Heaven and Mother Earth.*

Three produces wan wu. "Wan" means *ten thousand,* which represents *innumerable.* "Wu" means *thing.* "Wan wu" means *countless planets, stars, galaxies, and universes.*

Lao Zi's teaching that Tao creates One, One creates Two, Two creates Three, and Three creates countless planets, stars, galaxies, and universes is the process of Tao Normal Creation.

Tao Calligraphy is Oneness writing. It carries a Oneness field. When I write Tao Calligraphy, I was trained and given the sacred way from Tao Source to pour Tao Source shen qi jing into the calligraphy. Since I began writing Tao Calligraphy in 2013, it has created thousands of heart-touching and moving results for healing and transformation of health, relationships, finances, and more.

Why do people get sick? Why do people have relationship challenges? Why do people have financial challenges? Why do people have all kinds of challenges in life? I gave my insight in the introduction. I would like to emphasize it again. It can be summarized in one sentence:

All challenges in life, whether in health, relationships, or finances, are due to negative shen qi jing in soul, heart, mind, or body.

Why is Tao Calligraphy unique and powerful? This too can be summarized in one sentence:

Tao Calligraphy carries Tao Source positive shen qi jing that could transform negative shen qi jing in all life, including health, relationships, and finances.

All life includes:

- boosting energy, stamina, vitality, and immunity

- healing and transforming the physical, emotional, mental, and spiritual bodies
- healing and transforming all kinds of relationships
- healing and transforming finances and business
- opening spiritual communication channels
- increasing intelligence and wisdom
- enlightening the soul, heart, mind, and body

Tao Calligraphy is a new positive information system for healing and transformation to serve humanity in all life.

Many have experienced phenomenal results using Tao Calligraphy for healing and transformation. You can read about several examples in the appendix near the end of this book. My wish is for Tao Calligraphy to serve you, humanity, and Mother Earth much more.

Trace, chant, write Tao Calligraphy

As I just explained, Tao Calligraphy carries a field of Tao Source shen qi jing. This highest positive information shen qi jing field can transform any aspect of life because it can transform any negative shen qi jing in health, relationships, finances, and more.

To receive the benefits of Tao Calligraphy, one must do practices to connect with a Tao Calligraphy and receive its positive shen qi jing. I am including one Tao Calligraphy in chapter five of this book as a gift and will guide you there to use it in a practice.

There are three ways to practice with Tao Calligraphy: tracing, chanting, and writing.

Trace

Use one or both of two ways to trace: hand tracing and Dan tracing.

- **Hand tracing.** Put the five fingertips of one hand together. See figure 4. Now, using the Five Fingers tracing hand position, trace the Tao Calligraphy "Ai" (love) ten times. Figure 5 shows you the writing and tracing pathway of this Yi Bi Zi character.

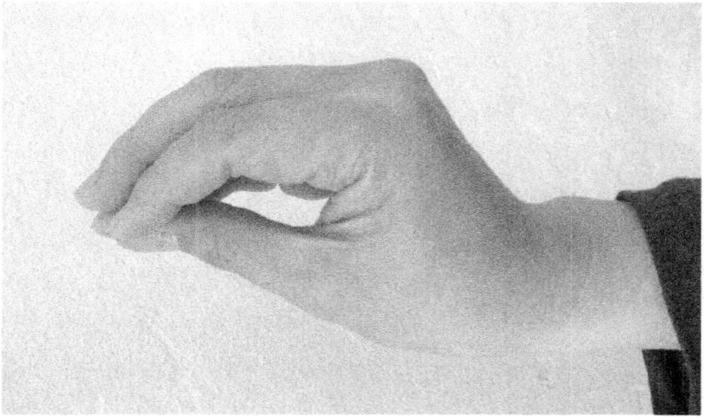

Figure 4. Five Fingers tracing hand position

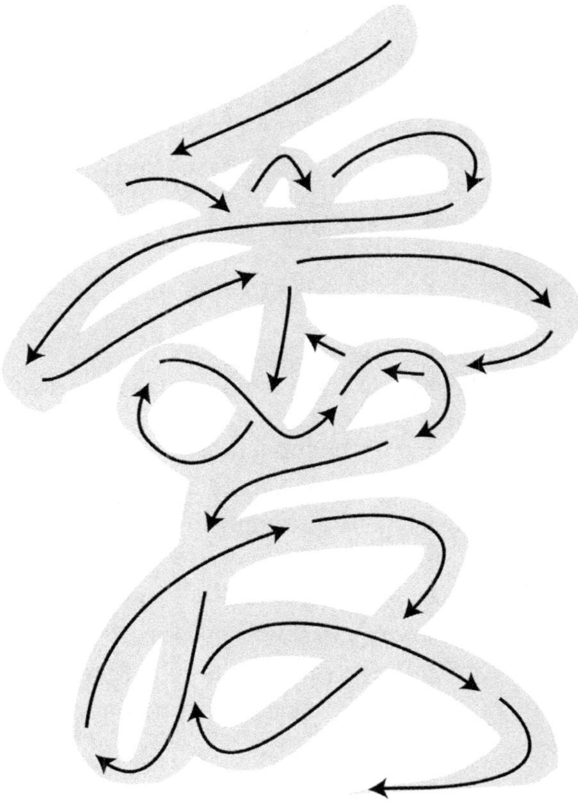

Figure 5. Tracing pathway of Tao Calligraphy “Ai” (love)

- **Dan tracing (Tao Calligraphy tai chi movement).** "Dan 丹" means *light ball.* Here, it specifically refers to a light ball in the lower abdomen, the location of the Lower Dan Tian, one of the body's foundational energy centers. ("Tian 田" means *field.*) A normal human being does not have this light ball, which is only formed through special energy and spiritual practices. Doing Tao Calligraphy tai chi movement through Dan tracing is a practice that could form your Dan. To form your Dan is to boost your energy, vitality, stamina, and immunity and to boost the healing and transformation of every aspect of your life.

  Stand with your feet shoulder width apart. Bend your knees and pelvic area slightly. Keep your back straight. Drop your shoulders and elbows. Gently touch the tip of your tongue to the roof of your mouth, with your chin tucked in slightly. Hold both palms facing each other about a foot apart in front of your lower abdomen, as though you were holding a volleyball or basketball. See figure 6.

  Dan tracing is to trace with your lower abdomen, the imaginary ball, your pelvic area, and your hips.

  The power and significance of tracing can be summarized in one sentence:

  What you trace is what you become.

  Now I will share one of the most important additional techniques when you do Dan tracing of Tao Calligraphy. Imagine there is a rope slightly lifting the top of your head, while at the same time your tailbone slightly drops. The spinal column naturally has an S-curve. This important visualization could straighten the spinal column, allowing energy to flow more freely through and around the spinal column. This is vital sacred wisdom and practice in ancient tai chi. It is absolutely a key for Tao Calligraphy tai chi movement also.

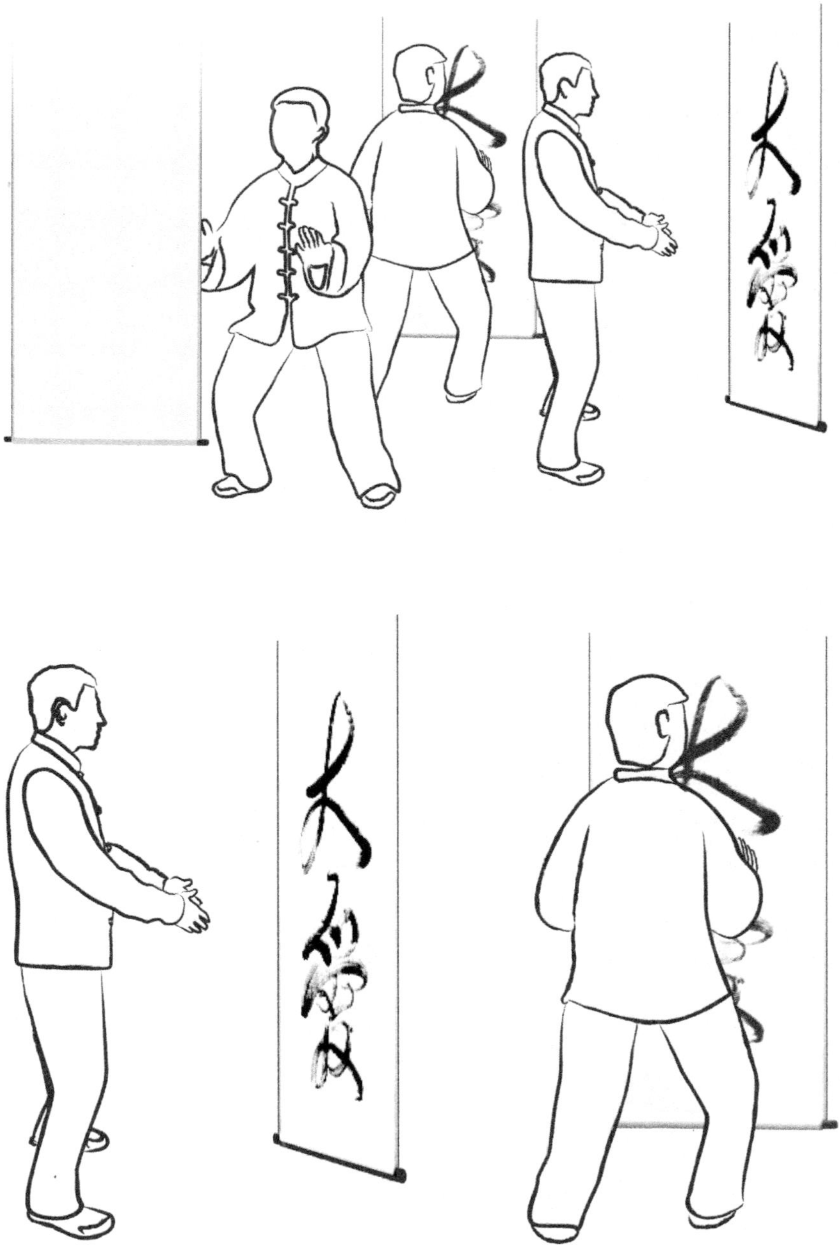

Figure 6. Dan tracing position

Why is this technique important? There is an ancient sacred and secret phrase:

wei lü zhong zheng shen guan ding
尾閭中正神灌頂

"Wei lü" means *tailbone*. "Zhong zheng" means *straight*. "Shen" means *Heaven and Tao*. "Guan ding" means *crown chakra*[4] *blessing*. "Wei lü zhong zheng shen guan ding" means *light pours into your crown chakra straight through the whole spinal column to the tailbone.*

Now, using the Dan tracing position, trace the Tao Calligraphy "Ai" (love) for a few minutes. (See figure 5 on page 7.) The imaginary ball between your hands traces the calligraphy along with your Dan. Your arms, hips, knees, and legs move together.

Chant

For thousands of years chanting has been one of the sacred techniques used in many spiritual and meditative practices. The power and significance of chanting can be summarized in one sentence:

What you chant is what you become.

Tao Calligraphy is a Source positive information system that carries Source positive shen qi jing. In the next chapter I will share the ten greatest qualities of Tao Source, which are the ten greatest qualities of a human being.

The first of the ten greatest qualities is Da Ai, *greatest love*. ("Da" means *greatest*. "Ai" means *love*.) In some of the practices in this book, we practice by chanting:

Da Ai (pronounced *dah eye*)
Da Ai
Da Ai
Da Ai ...

---

[4] See chapter eight for an introduction to the chakras.

Greatest love
Greatest love
Greatest love
Greatest love ...

To chant *Da Ai* or *greatest love* is to align with greatest love, to embody greatest love, and to become greatest love. I always teach: *Love melts all blockages and transforms all life.*

In all of the practices in this book, we will chant this and other positive Tao Source messages or special healing, transformational, and empowering sacred sounds.

Write

There are two ways to write Tao Calligraphy:

- **Write on water-writing cloths.** This is the basic beginning way to write Tao Calligraphy. These cloths are for practicing calligraphy writing using a brush and water rather than ink. When the water evaporates, the writing disappears, and the cloth can be used again and again. I have created water paper with outlines of various Tao Calligraphies imprinted on them. See figure 7. You can write over the imprints on the water-writing cloth. These water-writing cloths are used in special training to develop Tao Calligraphy Practitioners and Tao Calligraphy Teachers. The best way to learn to write Tao Calligraphy is to repeatedly trace or write over a water-writing cloth imprint dozens of times before actually using a brush, ink, and blank calligraphy paper.

- **Write on blank calligraphy paper with brush and ink.** This is the advanced way to write Tao Calligraphy. I do not recommend that you do this without special training from my Tao Calligraphy Teachers or me.

The power and significance of writing Tao Calligraphy can be summarized in one sentence:

What you write is what you become.

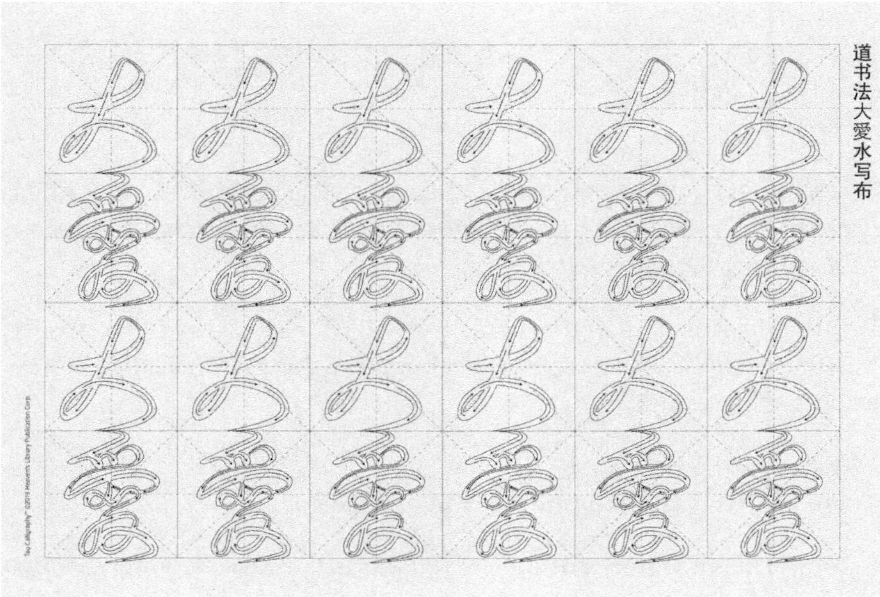

Figure 7. Tao Calligraphy *Da Ai* water-writing cloth

ꙮ

You can trace, chant, or write Tao Calligraphy by yourself or with others. Tracing, chanting, or writing by yourself is self-healing and transformation. Tracing, chanting, or writing with others is group healing and transformation. In general, group healing is more powerful than self-healing because the group (two or more people) is aligning and focusing their healing and transformational practice.

A single Tao Calligraphy is a Tao Calligraphy healing field because it carries Tao Source positive shen qi jing. The Tao Calligraphy healing fields in my Tao Centers worldwide are created by thirty to more than one hundred Tao Calligraphies. When you trace, chant, or write Tao Calligraphies, you are connecting with the Tao Calligraphy healing field. You will understand how to make a deep connection through six sacred

Tao power techniques that you will learn in chapter three and apply in the practices thereafter.

Tracing, chanting, and writing Tao Calligraphy are to connect with an external Tao Calligraphy healing field to bring the field's Tao Source positive shen qi jing to you to remove or transform your negative shen qi jing.

It is also possible to receive and connect with an internal Tao Calligraphy field.

Tao Calligraphy Light Field transmissions from a Tao Calligraphy

Specially trained and certified Tao Calligraphy Healing Field Grandmaster and Master Healers and Teachers can offer Tao Shen Qi Jing Light Fields from Tao Calligraphies to a person, a pet, and more.

If, for example, you have pain or other challenges in your back, a Tao Calligraphy Healing Field Master Healer and Teacher has the honor and ability to transmit a light field for the back to you from a Tao Calligraphy. Once you receive such a transmission, this Tao Calligraphy Light Field becomes an *internal* Tao Calligraphy healing field for your back that you can access and connect with anywhere, anytime. The transmission will always remain with you.

To receive continued benefits from a Tao Calligraphy Light Field transmitted for your back, you simply connect by "saying *hello*" (Soul Power is explained in chapter three) and chanting repeatedly:

Tao Calligraphy Back Light Field
Tao Calligraphy Back Light Field
Tao Calligraphy Back Light Field
Tao Calligraphy Back Light Field …

I have trained about thirty Tao Calligraphy Healing Field Grandmaster and Master Healers and Teachers who can offer this unique Tao Source service. More are on the way. It is very powerful to receive and carry one or more of these internal Tao Calligraphy healing fields. If you have serious, chronic, or life-threatening health or other challenges, I strongly encourage you to learn more about Tao Calligraphy Light Field transmissions from any of my trained and certified Tao Calligraphy Healing Field Master Healers and Teachers.

2

Ten Greatest Qualities of Tao Source

TAO SOURCE HAS GIVEN me Ten Greatest Qualities. These qualities are called Shi Da (十大). "Shi" means *ten*. "Da" means *greatest*. Shi Da means *ten greatest*.

What are the Ten Greatest Qualities?

Lao Zi, in his timeless classic *Dao De Jing*, wrote, "There are four Da in countless planets, stars, galaxies, and universes." They are:

道大　Dao da
天大　tian da
地大　di da
人大　ren da

The first of Lao Zi's four Da is Dao da. Tao is *the Source*. "Dao da" means *the Source is greatest*. Tao is the ultimate Creator. Tao creates everyone and everything. De nourishes everyone and everything. "De 德" is the *virtue of Tao*, which is manifest in the *shen kou yi of Tao*. "Shen 身" means *actions, activities, and behaviors*. "Kou 口" means *speech*. "Yi 意" means *thoughts*.

In summary:

Tao is the ultimate Source and Way of all life.
De is the actions, activities, and behaviors of Tao.

The second of Lao Zi's four Da is tian da. "Tian" means *Heaven*. "Tian da" means *Heaven is greatest*. In Lao Zi's concept, Heaven includes the sun, moon, solar system, Big Dipper, Milky Way, and universe. Heaven includes countless solar systems, galaxies, and universes. Heaven shines and nourishes everyone and everything.

The third of Lao Zi's four Da is di da. "Di" means *Mother Earth*. "Di da" means *Mother Earth is greatest*.

Mother Earth has the greatest heart. She holds everyone and everything (wan wu 萬物, literally *ten thousand things*, which signifies *innumerable things* in Chinese).

There is an ancient saying:

hou de zai wu
厚德載物

"Hou" means *thick*, which indicates *a great deal*. "De" again is *the virtue that comes from Tao through the shen kou yi of Tao*. "Zai" means *to carry*. "Wu" means *things*. "Wan wu" includes everyone and everything in Mother Earth. "Hou de zai wu" means *with great virtue one can hold the world*. Mother Earth raises and nourishes wan wu. It takes great virtue to hold everyone and everything. Mother Earth does not distinguish whether a person offers positive service or negative service. Therefore, Mother Earth has great de.

Mother Earth has the biggest heart. Therefore, Mother Earth is one of the greatest.

The fourth of Lao Zi's four Da is ren da. "Ren" means *human being*. "Ren da" means *human being is greatest*. Another ancient statement is:

ren wei wan wu zhi ling
人為萬物之靈

"Wei" means *is*. "Zhi" acts like an apostrophe to denote a possessive. "Ling" means *smartest*. "Ren wei wan wu zhi ling" means *human beings are the smartest within countless planets, stars, galaxies, and universes*.

Human beings create and manifest throughout history to improve life. Human beings evolve constantly. Therefore, human beings are one of the greatest.

In fact, "da 大" has three key meanings:

- greatest
- unconditional
- selfless

Therefore, the Ten Da, Shi Da, or Ten Greatest Qualities are actually the ten greatest, unconditional, and selfless qualities.

Power and significance of the Ten Greatest Qualities

In two of my earlier books, *Soul Over Matter*[5] and *Tao Classic of Longevity and Immortality*,[6] I explained the sacred deep wisdom of the Ten Da and gave detailed practices to gain the Ten Da. I will not repeat those teachings in this book, but I will share the essence of each Da, each greatest quality, now.

Greatest Love—Da Ai (大愛)

Four sacred phrases explain Da Ai, *greatest love*:

yi shi Da Ai	一施大愛
wu tiao jian ai	無條件愛
rong hua zai nan	融化災難
xin qing shen ming	心清神明

First give greatest love, the first of the Ten Da natures of Tao.
Unconditional love

[5] Dr. and Master Zhi Gang Sha and Adam Markel, *Soul Over Matter: Ancient and Modern Wisdom and Practical Techniques to Create Unlimited Abundance*, Dallas, TX/Toronto, ON: BenBella Books/Heaven's Library Publication Corp., 2017.

[6] Dr. and Master Zhi Gang Sha, *Tao Classic of Longevity and Immortality: Sacred Wisdom and Practical Techniques*, Cardiff, CA/Richmond Hill, ON: Waterside Press/Heaven's Library Publication Corp., 2019.

Melts all blockages.
Heart clear; soul, heart, and mind enlightened.

Everyone has their own beliefs. Many believe in science. Many believe in spirituality. Some believe in their own way. Regardless, everyone needs the greatest love.

Think about your life. Have you received love from your parents? Have you received love from your children? Have you received love from your partners? Have you received love from your colleagues? When you feel love, what is that feeling like? When you do not feel love, what is that feeling like? I want to share that love is the quality and feeling that not only all of humanity needs, but that all animals, nature, the environment, and more need as well.

These four sacred phrases explain very clearly that when you give the greatest, unconditional, selfless love to yourself and others, all kinds of life blockages, including in health, relationships, finances, and every aspect of life, could be removed. Da Ai can clear your heart and enlighten your soul, heart, mind, and body.

I have placed a Tao Calligraphy *Da Ai* on the back cover of this book.

Greatest Forgiveness—Da Kuan Shu（大寬恕）

Da Kuan Shu, *greatest forgiveness*, is the second of the Ten Da natures of Tao. The four-line sacred Tao mantra of Da Kuan Shu is:

er Da Kuan Shu	二大寬恕
wo yuan liang ni	我原諒你
ni yuan liang wo	你原諒我
xiang ai ping an he xie	相愛平安和諧

The second of the Ten Da natures of Tao is greatest forgiveness.
I forgive you.
You forgive me.
Love, peace, and harmony.

Human beings could have the following challenges in life:

- health challenges, including all kinds of pain, infections, cysts, tumors, cancer, and more
- emotional challenges, including anger, depression, anxiety, worry, grief, fear, guilt, and more
- mental challenges, including all kinds of mental disorders, mental confusion, poor memory, and more
- spiritual challenges, including lack of direction for the spiritual journey and more
- all kinds of relationship challenges, including with family members, relatives, colleagues, and more
- all kinds of financial and business challenges

Deep spiritual wisdom teaches that all challenges are related with soul, heart, mind, energy, and matter blockages. Practicing forgiveness could create amazing transformation of one's challenges beyond comprehension.

Think about your family. A husband and wife could argue and fight. Partners, parents and children, and more could argue and fight. How can you bring love, peace, and harmony? If person A and person B have issues, what if A sincerely apologized to B or B sincerely apologized to A? The issues could be resolved very quickly.

Expanding the wisdom, if any employees in a workplace have challenges with one another, what if they could sincerely apologize to each other? Then, the situation could become very positive.

I have shared the sacred forgiveness teachings and practice with thousands of students and clients worldwide:

I forgive you.
You forgive me.
Bring love, peace, and harmony.

Doing forgiveness practice could yield unbelievable results. People may not understand that health challenges, relationship blockages, and even financial issues are very closely related with the emotions. If you have emotional imbalances, your health, relationships, or finances could be deeply affected. Therefore, to do forgiveness with anyone with whom you have challenges could bring truly remarkable results.

If you know you have challenges with someone, do a forgiveness practice with the person directly if you can.

You can also do a general forgiveness practice for any or all of your challenges. For example, if you have knee pain, suffer from anxiety, have financial challenges, or for all of your life challenges, you can do a general forgiveness practice as follows:

> *Dear everyone and everything with whom I have had any conflict, argument, or fighting regarding anything that I am aware of or even not aware of, I honor you. Please let us do a forgiveness practice together.*

Then, repeatedly chant:

> *I forgive you.*
> *You forgive me.*
> *Bring love, peace, and harmony.*

Spend five to ten minutes repeating these three sentences. You could feel remarkable improvement. You could feel some improvement. You could feel no improvement. Whether you feel remarkable improvement, some improvement, or no improvement, continue to do the forgiveness practice sincerely three times a day for five to ten minutes each time for a few days. Then, see how you feel.

This is very simple but it is a very sacred way to do forgiveness practice to transform your health, relationship, or financial challenges. Try it. Experience it.

Forgiveness is the golden key to unlock all life challenges. Between family member and family member, colleague and colleague, organization and organization, and country and country, if there are any conflicts, arguments, fighting, or more, applying forgiveness could help to transform the condition beyond words.

Humanity and Mother Earth truly need much more forgiveness in order to bring love, peace, and harmony in health, relationships, finances, and every aspect of life.

Greatest Compassion—Da Ci Bei (大慈悲)

Da Ci Bei, *greatest compassion,* is the third of the Ten Da natures of Tao. The sacred four-line Tao mantra of Da Ci Bei is:

san Da Ci Bei 三大慈悲
yuan li zeng qiang 願力增强
fu wu zhong sheng 服務眾生
gong de wu liang 功德無量

The third of the Ten Da natures of Tao is greatest compassion.
Increase and strengthen willpower.
Serve humanity and all souls.
Gain immeasurable virtue.

Millions of people honor Mother Mary and Guan Yin, the Compassion Buddha. They are both universal mothers who have unconditional love and compassion for humanity and all souls.

Greatest compassion is the highest and unconditional compassion. There are many heart-touching stories of Guan Yin and Mother Mary transforming hopeless conditions and saving lives. Call and connect with them to receive their love and compassion.

Greatest Light—Da Guang Ming (大光明)

Da Guang Ming, *greatest light,* is the fourth of the Ten Da natures of Tao. The sacred four-line Tao Source mantra of Da Guang Ming is:

si Da Guang Ming 四大光明
wo zai Dao guang zhong 我在道光中
Dao guang zai wo zhong 道光在我中
tong ti tou ming 通體透明

The fourth of the Ten Da natures of Tao is greatest light and transparency.
I am inside Tao Source light.
Tao Source light is inside me.
The whole body is completely light and transparent.

Tao is the ultimate Source. If you are inside Tao Source light and Tao Source light is inside you, then you are in the Tao Source light field. This is a beyond powerful practice to heal and transform every aspect of life.

A human being has a human being's shen qi jing, which are one's soul, heart, mind, and body. Tao light has Source shen qi jing, which are Source soul, heart, mind, and body. Tao light can transform our human light beyond any comprehension. Therefore, Da Guang Ming, greatest light, is a sacred way to heal and transform all life.

Greatest Humility—Da Qian Bei (大謙卑)

Da Qian Bei, *greatest humility*, is the fifth of the Ten Da natures of Tao. The sacred Tao Source mantra of Da Qian Bei has five lines:

wu Da Qian Bei	五大謙卑
rou ruo bu zheng	柔弱不爭
chi xu jing jin	持續精進
shi qian bei	失謙卑
die wan zhang	跌萬丈

The fifth of the Ten Da natures of Tao is greatest humility.
Be gentle and soft, do not compete or fight.
Improve persistently.
Lose humility
Fail tremendously in every aspect of life, just like falling into a deep cavern.

Humility benefits life and prevents disasters and challenges. Ego is one of the biggest blockages in every aspect of life.

Lao Zi's *Dao De Jing* emphasizes the importance of humility. I would like to share a few chapters of *Dao De Jing*.

Chapter 7 of *Dao De Jing* states:

> *Heaven and Mother Earth have long, long lives. Why? Because Heaven and Mother Earth follow nature's way and serve unconditionally and selflessly. They do not live for themselves. Therefore, the person who has gained Tao wisdom always lets others shine in the front while staying in the background. In fact, others respect the one who stays behind more. Such a person can give their life to serve others. Then, this one can stay much longer. Because this one is selfless and has no ego, this one will naturally achieve the true life purpose and goal.*

This chapter is a powerful teaching about the wisdom and blessings of humility.

Chapter 8 of *Dao De Jing* states:

> *The highest Tao and de* (actions, speech, and thoughts of Tao) *are like water. Water nourishes countless things and does not fight with anyone or anything. Water stays in the lowest places that others may not like. Therefore, water is closest to Tao.*

This is another teaching of the selfless yin nature of humility.

Chapter 24 of *Dao De Jing* states:

> *The person who often shows off cannot truly shine. The person who thinks that they are always correct cannot discern the truth. The people who admire themselves cannot truly be successful. The people who have ego cannot last long.*

I believe ego is the biggest enemy for one's journey of healing and transformation, as well as for one's spiritual journey.

The eighty-first and final chapter of *Dao De Jing* states:

> *The saints do not have a heart to control others, but only serve others unconditionally. As a result, the saints flourish more. The saints give to others the most. As a result, the saints have more abundance. The Tao of Heaven is to let everyone and everything flourish more and to not harm anyone or anything. The Tao of saints is not to argue or fight with others.*

This teaching reflects the truth of "she de 捨得," *give to receive*. The more you give, the more you will receive. Give and serve unconditionally and selflessly like the great saints and Heaven's unlimited blessings could be showered on your health, relationships, finances, and every aspect of your life.

The above teachings and wisdom in Lao Zi's *Dao De Jing* have truly emphasized the power and significance of Da Qian Bei.

Greatest Harmony—Da He Xie（大和諧）

Da He Xie, *greatest harmony*, is the sixth of the Ten Da natures of Tao. It is another essential quality for true success in one's life. The four-line sacred Tao mantra of Da He Xie is:

liu Da He Xie 六大和諧
san ren tong xin 三人同心
qi li duan jin 齊力斷金
cheng gong mi jue 成功秘訣

The sixth of the Ten Da natures of Tao is greatest harmony.
Three people join hearts together.
Their strength can cut gold.
The secret of success.

To have a happy family, each family member must offer love, care, and compassion. Everyone needs to forgive each other and be in harmony.

An ancient saying is jia he wan shi xing (家和萬事興). "Jia" means *family*. "He" means *harmony*. "Wan" means *ten thousand*. It represents a "myriad" or "innumerable" in Chinese. "Shi" means *things*. "Xing" means *flourishing*. "Jia he wan shi xing" means *in a harmonized family everything flourishes*.

Think about a very successful business. It must have a great harmonized team. Da He Xie represents great teamwork. Without Da He Xie, it is impossible to have great flourishing. To have greatest harmony, one must also have the other Ten Da natures.

The Ten Da are the natures of Tao, buddhas, saints, the Divine, Mother Earth, countless planets, stars, galaxies, and universes, and human beings. Da He Xie is great teamwork, which is the key for success. Let us love one another and join hearts as one to create greatest success in every aspect of our lives.

Greatest Flourishing—Da Chang Sheng (大昌盛)

Da Chang Sheng, *greatest flourishing*, is the seventh of the Ten Da natures of Tao. The four-line sacred Tao Source mantra of Da Chang Sheng is:

qi Da Chang Sheng	七大昌盛
Dao ci ying fu	道賜盈福
xing shan ji de	行善積德
Dao ye chang sheng	道業昌盛

The seventh of the Ten Da natures of Tao is greatest flourishing.
Tao Source bestows huge prosperity, luck, and success.
Offer kind service to accumulate virtue.
Tao career flourishes.

I would like to share a deep spiritual wisdom. The roots of a person's flourishing are the positive information system of the person's positive shen qi jing, which are the positive information or messages carried by one's soul, heart, mind, and body, from past lifetimes and the current lifetime. If you have open spiritual communication channels, you may be able to see some past lifetimes to understand this truth.

Financial success is due to positive shen qi jing messages from your ancestors and yourself from past and current lifetimes and your great personal effort in the current lifetime. Positive shen qi jing information or messages are accumulated through great positive service for humanity, animals, the environment, and more. Positive service is to make humanity, animals, and the environment healthier and happier and to transform them in a positive way. These positive shen qi jing messages can bless your financial flourishing in your current lifetime and in future lifetimes.

If you have great flourishing, congratulations. I wish for you to receive more. If you do not have great flourishing, how can you create it? The secret is to strengthen your system of positive information: accumulate positive shen qi jing information or messages through shen, kou, and yi (action, speech, and thought).

In chapter three, I will explain in detail the six sacred Tao power techniques that are the core of every practice for healing and transformation in the remainder of this book. To apply the six sacred Tao power techniques, of which tracing Tao Source Calligraphies is one, is to accumulate positive shen qi jing information or messages.

Let me share an example. A businessman in Los Angeles received one of my Tao Calligraphies, "Dao Ye Chang Sheng 道業昌盛," the fourth line of the sacred Tao Source mantra of greatest flourishing. Less than two years later, he told me, "Since I received the 'Dao Ye Chang Sheng' [*Tao career flourishes*] Tao Calligraphy, I have traced it while chanting for about ten minutes every day. Money keeps coming without any effort. Everything is flowing. My company has grown from a two-million-dollar business to sixty million dollars within two years. I absolutely give the credit to the 'Dao Ye Chang Sheng' Tao Calligraphy and mantra."

Because the "Dao Ye Chang Sheng" Tao Calligraphy and mantra carry positive shen qi jing messages of Tao Source, this man's business received huge blessings from these Tao messages.

Greatest Gratitude—Da Gan En（大感恩）

Da Gan En, *greatest gratitude*, is the eighth of the Ten Da natures of Tao. The four-line sacred Tao mantra of Da Gan En can transform our lives further and enhance every aspect of our lives:

ba Da Gan En	八大感恩
Dao sheng de yang	道生德養
zai pei ci hui	栽培賜慧
Dao en yong cun	道恩永存

The eighth of the Ten Da natures of Tao is greatest gratitude.
Tao Source creates all things and de nourishes them.
Tao Source cultivates and bestows wisdom and intelligence.
The glory of Tao Source should remain in our hearts and souls forever.

In our lives there are many people who have helped us physically or spiritually. We should always show our gratitude to them. Parents raise their children. Children should have gratitude for their parents. Teachers in kindergarten, elementary school, middle school, high school, and university teach their students. Students should express gratitude to their teachers.

The Divine and Tao Source have bestowed appropriate wisdom and blessings to every soul's physical life and spiritual journey. We should be grateful and show appreciation to them.

Gratitude is one of the Tao natures that every human being and every soul should have. For our good health, happiness, harmonious relationships, and financial and business flourishing, we need to show our gratitude to the Divine, Tao Source, and anyone who has helped us on our spiritual or physical journeys.

Greatest Service—Da Fu Wu（大服務）

Da Fu Wu, *greatest service,* is the ninth of the Ten Da natures of Tao. I always share with my students and humanity that the purpose of life is to serve. To serve is to make others happier and healthier, as well as successful in every aspect of their lives and our own lives.

The four-line sacred Tao mantra of Da Fu Wu is:

jiu Da Fu Wu	九大服務
shi wei gong pu	誓為公僕
wu si feng xian	無私奉獻
shang cheng fa men	上乘法門

The ninth of the Ten Da natures of Tao is greatest service.
Vow to be a servant of humanity and all souls.

Selflessly offer service.
The highest way to reach Tao Source.

I would like to share a personal story from my spiritual journey. Many years ago, I was in Taiwan. Shakyamuni Buddha, honored as the founder of Buddhism, appeared to me one day during my meditation. He is one of my spiritual fathers forever. I asked him, "Shi Jia Mo Ni Fo (釋迦牟尼佛, his name in Chinese), you taught eighty-four thousand methods of xiu lian[7] (修煉) in order to reach Buddhahood, which is the highest enlightenment. Of these eighty-four thousand xiu lian methods, what is the highest method?" He responded, "What do you think?" I said, "I feel the number one method for the xiu lian journey is service xiu lian, which means to serve others, to make others happier and healthier." He smiled at me and said, "I couldn't agree with you enough."

Service has layers. You can serve a little, serve more, or serve unconditionally. To serve unconditionally is the highest way to progress on your spiritual journey.

Greatest Enlightenment—Da Yuan Man (大圓滿)

Da Yuan Man, *greatest enlightenment*, is the tenth of the Ten Da natures of Tao. It is the last Tao nature required to align completely with and reach Tao. The four-line sacred Tao mantra of Da Yuan Man is:

shi Da Yuan Man	十大圓滿
ling xin nao shen yuan man	靈心腦身圓滿
ren di tian Dao shen xian ti	人地天道神仙梯
fu wu xiu lian cai ke pan	服務修煉才可攀

The tenth Da nature of Tao is greatest enlightenment.
Soul, heart, mind, and body enlightenment

---

[7] "Xiu" means *purification*. "Lian" means *practice*. "Xiu lian" means *purification practice to transform our negative shen qi jing messages to positive shen qi jing messages in all conditions, smooth and difficult*. Therefore, xiu lian is practice to heal and transform one's soul, heart, mind, and body. It is practice to serve one's physical and spiritual journeys.

Levels of saint servants: ren xian, di xian, tian xian, and Tao xian[8]
Only through service can greatest enlightenment be achieved.

There are three essences of traditional Chinese culture: Buddhism, Taoism, and Confucianism. In Chinese philosophy, they are called san jiao (三教 three doctrines), considered as a harmonious unit. The highest achievement in Buddhism is to reach the highest enlightenment, which is to reach Buddhahood. The highest achievement of enlightenment in Taoism is to become immortal. The highest achievement of enlightenment in Confucianism is to become the highest saint.

There are many other spiritual belief systems, including Christianity, Islam, Hinduism, Judaism, Sikhism, indigenous, and more. In general, the highest achievement of enlightenment in each of these belief systems is to reach the highest saint in their realm.

The highest saints who have reached the highest enlightenment have completely removed negative shen qi jing information or messages in order to completely embody the Ten Da qualities in every aspect of their lives and maintain these qualities at all times. These Ten Da qualities are the highest positive messages. They form the highest positive information system. These Ten Da qualities are the nature of buddhas, immortals, and highest saints.

A human being has both positive information or messages and negative information or messages in their shen qi jing. A human being's spiritual journey is to accumulate positive shen qi jing messages and remove negative shen qi jing messages. What is life about? It can be summarized in one sentence:

Life is to transform negative shen qi jing messages to positive shen qi jing messages.

---

[8] Ren xian, di xian, tian xian, and Tao xian are ascending levels of saint servants. They mean Human saint, Mother Earth saint, Heaven saint, and Tao saint, respectively. A Human saint can harmonize and transform humanity. A Mother Earth saint can harmonize and transform Mother Earth. A Heaven saint can harmonize and transform Heaven. A Tao saint has the extraordinary abilities of Tao Source.

What are negative shen qi jing messages? Negative shen qi jing messages are negative soul, heart, mind, energy, and matter messages.

Negative soul messages are the information from mistakes one and one's ancestors have made in all lifetimes. These mistakes can include killing, harming, taking advantage of others, cheating, stealing, and more.

Negative heart messages include tan (貪 greed), chen (嗔 anger), chi (痴 lack of wisdom in actions, activities, behaviors, speech, and thoughts), man (慢 ego), yi (疑 doubt), ming li (名利 desire for fame and wealth), selfishness, impurities, and more.

Negative mind messages include negative mindsets, negative beliefs, negative attitudes, ego, attachments, and more.

Negative energy messages are located between the cells and organs in the spaces of the human body. They include excess energy, insufficient energy, blocked energy, mislocated energy, and more.

Negative matter messages are located inside the cells and organs of the human body. They include improper growths, misalignments, insufficient matter, irregularities in DNA or RNA, and more.

Relationships, finances, and every aspect of life can also carry negative soul, heart, mind, energy, and matter messages. If you have challenges in relationships, finances, or any aspect of life, then that aspect has negative soul, heart, mind, energy, or matter information or messages.

Millions and millions of people throughout history have searched for and practiced to reach the highest achievement of enlightenment. Millions of people have studied, respected, and honored great buddhas, immortals, and highest saints in all kinds of spiritual realms. I wish more people could reach the highest achievement of enlightenment.

3

Six Sacred Tao Power Techniques

TAO SOURCE TECHNIQUES FOR healing and transformation have been given to humanity in history. They have been used, for example, for thousands of years in Chinese energy and spiritual practices. In this chapter, I summarize and share with humanity the six most important sacred Tao power techniques, which are:

- Body Power
- Soul Power
- Mind Power
- Sound Power
- Breath Power
- Tao Calligraphy Power

In subsequent chapters, we will apply these six sacred power techniques in many practices to transform all life.

Body Power

Body Power is to use hand and body positions to purify and to remove negative shen qi jing messages in order to heal, boost energy, rejuvenate, prolong life, transform relationships and finances, and more.

Throughout history, humanity has used many different body and hand positions that carry Body Power. Consider, for example, the many mudras used in Hinduism, Buddhism, yoga, Indian dance, and more. They are symbolic poses or gestures that can use the whole body or just the hands and fingers. Many mudras carry profound spiritual significance and power and can be seen in many artistic depictions of the great saints and buddhas in many traditions.

The essence of the simple Body Power technique that I will apply most often in this book can be described in one sentence:

Where you put your hands is where you receive healing and transformation.

Soul Power

Soul Power is to make a soul-to-soul, heart-to-heart connection by saying *hello* to Tao Source, Heaven, Mother Earth, nature, the sun and moon, and countless planets, stars, galaxies, and universes, as well as to all realms of spiritual fathers and mothers—saints and buddhas—that you believe in. Soul Power is also to say *hello* to inner souls, including the souls of your systems, organs, parts of the body, cells, spaces, and more.

The sacred practice and wisdom of Soul Power can be summarized in one sentence:

Whom and what you connect with and say *hello* to is whose healing and blessing you receive.

Mind Power

Mind Power is creative visualization. Many teachers have taught many great visualization techniques. One of the most powerful Mind Power practices is to visualize golden light radiating in your body, relationships, or finances. There is an ancient saying: jin guang zhao ti, bai bing xiao chu (金光照體，百病消除). "Jin" means *gold*. "Guang" means *light*. "Zhao" means *to shine*. "Ti" means *body*. "Bai" means *one hundred*, which can represent *numerous* or *all kinds*. "Bing" means *sickness*. "Xiao chu" means *to remove*. So, "jin guang zhao ti, bai bing xiao chu" means *golden light shines in the body, all sicknesses are removed.*

Mind Power can be summarized in one sentence:

What you visualize is what you become.

Sound Power

Sound Power is to chant or sing sacred mantras. A mantra is a healing and transformational sound or message to be chanted or sung repeatedly. There are many sacred mantras for healing and transformation. They can range in length from one syllable ("Om") to hundreds of lines of text with syntax and meaning.

Sound Power can be summarized in one sentence:

What you chant is what you become.

Breath Power

Breath Power is to use special breathing techniques.

There are many breathing techniques. Many are taught for the purposes of relieving stress, boosting energy, or simply improving lung function. The yogic practice of breath control called pranayama is one of the most renowned ancient practices that is still in common use.

Breath Power can be summarized in one sentence:

Different breathing techniques are to develop, heal, and transform different parts of the body.

Tao Calligraphy Power

As I explained in chapter one, Tao Calligraphy Power is to trace, chant, or write Tao Calligraphy.

Tao Calligraphy has no limit. Tao Calligraphy carries Tao Source positive shen qi jing that could transform negative shen qi jing in all life, including health, relationships, and finances.

Therefore, Tao Calligraphies can be written that can help:

- boost energy, stamina, vitality, and immunity
- heal and transform the physical, emotional, mental, or spiritual bodies
- heal and transform all kinds of relationships
- heal and transform finances and business
- open spiritual communication channels
- increase intelligence and wisdom
- enlighten the soul, heart, mind, and body
- and more

Tao Calligraphy Power can be summarized in one sentence:

What you trace, chant, or write in Tao Calligraphy is what you become.

Six powers join as one

To apply any one of the six sacred power techniques is powerful. To apply all six sacred power techniques together is extremely powerful. To apply all six sacred power techniques as one could bring additional Tao Source positive shen qi jing more quickly to your health, relationships, finances, and every aspect of your life.

In this book, I will guide you to use all six sacred Tao power techniques together to heal and transform every aspect of life.

Forgiveness

Forgiveness is a key part of Soul Power within the six sacred Tao power techniques. Forgiveness is powerful spiritual and energy healing for all blockages—physical, emotional, mental, and spiritual—in health, relationships, and finances. Forgive anyone who bothers you, harms you, or has a conflict with you. If you can offer unconditional forgiveness to those who hurt or bothered you, you could receive incredible blessings of healing and transformation.

Why is this so? People who have hurt you leave a negative message of that hurt on your soul, on your heart, on your subconscious mind, on your conscious mind, and on the soul, heart, mind, and body of your organs and cells. That negative message will affect cellular vibration, causing the transformation between matter inside the cells and energy outside the cells to go out of balance. This imbalance causes sickness. If you can offer the blessing of total, unconditional forgiveness to those who have hurt you, divine light and love will wash away the message of the hurt imprinted on your soul, heart, mind, organs, and cells. That is why forgiveness can heal existing sickness and why it could prevent sickness from occurring.

It is also vital to ask for forgiveness from those whom you have hurt. When those you have hurt or harmed grant you forgiveness, you are released from their anger, vengefulness, and more. The imprint of hurt needs to be released from both sides for healing and transformation to be complete. Both you and the other are healed and transformed. Your relationship is also healed and transformed.

Unconditional forgiveness is easy to say but difficult to do. The more you can truly offer unconditional forgiveness, the more healing could happen immediately. The potential healing blessings are unlimited.

You do not need to simply heed my words. The physical and emotional benefits of forgiveness have been confirmed scientifically. Research indicates that forgiveness reduces stress caused by the unbalanced emotions of bitterness, anger, and fear. As an ancient sage once said, "Before you embark on a journey of revenge, dig two graves."

4

Healing and Transformation with the Five Elements

IN TRADITIONAL CHINESE MEDICINE, Five Elements (wu xing 五行) is one of the most important theories and practices. Colleges of traditional Chinese medicine offer very deep teachings on the Five Elements.

Five Elements is one of the major universal laws. Its significance and power cannot be emphasized enough.

What are the Five Elements?

The five elements of nature (Wood 木, Fire 火, Earth 土, Metal 金, Water 水) summarize and categorize a human being's internal organs, sensory organs, bodily tissues and fluids, emotional body, and more. Bodily systems, organs, and cells can all be categorized into the five elements. Balancing the five elements is one of the keys to healing in traditional Chinese medicine. Five Elements theory has guided millions of people in history to heal sickness and to rejuvenate soul, heart, mind, and body.

Expanding the wisdom, there are countless planets in the universe. They can be categorized into Wood planets, Fire planets, Earth planets, Metal planets, and Water planets.

Countless stars, galaxies, and universes can also be categorized into the five elements. Balancing the five elements is one of the keys to healing for countless planets, stars, galaxies, and universes.

Figure 8 below shows how key bodily organs, sensory organs, tissues, fluids, and emotions are categorized by the five elements.

Wood element

The Wood element includes the liver, gallbladder, eyes, tendons, and nails in the physical body, anger in the emotional body, and more.

Fire element

The Fire element includes the heart, small intestine, tongue, and all blood vessels in the physical body, anxiety and depression in the emotional body, and more.

Element	Yin Organ (zang)	Yang Organ (fu)	Body Tissue	Body Fluid	Sense	Unbal-anced Emotion	Balanced Emotion
Wood	Liver	Gall-bladder	Tendons Nails	Tears	Eyes Sight	Anger	Patience
Fire	Heart	Small Intestine	Blood Vessels	Sweat	Tongue Taste	Depression Anxiety Excitability	Joy
Earth	Spleen	Stomach	Muscles	Saliva	Mouth Lips Speech	Worry	Love Compas-sion
Metal	Lungs	Large Intestine	Skin	Mucus	Nose Smell	Grief Sadness	Courage
Water	Kidneys	Urinary Bladder	Bones Joints	Urine	Ears Hearing	Fear	Calmness

Figure 8. Five Elements in the physical and emotional bodies

Earth element

The Earth element includes the spleen, stomach, mouth, lips, gums, teeth, and muscles in the physical body, worry in the emotional body, and more.

Metal element

The Metal element includes the lungs, large intestine, nose, and skin in the physical body, sadness and grief in the emotional body, and more.

Water element

The Water element includes the kidneys, urinary bladder, ears, bones, and joints in the physical body, fear in the emotional body, and more.

Figure 9 below shows further categories of the Five Elements, including several for the external environment.

Element	Finger	Taste	Colour	Weather	Season	Direction	Phase	Energy
Wood	Index	Sour	Green	Windy	Spring	East	New Yang	Genera-tive
Fire	Middle	Bitter	Red	Hot	Summer	South	Full Yang	Expan-sive
Earth	Thumb	Sweet	Yellow	Damp	Change of Seasons	Central	Yin/Yang Balance	Stabiliz-ing
Metal	Ring	Pungent Umami	White	Dry	Autumn	West	New Yin	Contract-ing
Water	Little	Salty	Blue	Cold	Winter	North	Full Yin	Conserv-ing

Figure 9. Five Elements in nature and more

Power and significance of the Five Elements for healing and transformation

Just as all parts of our physical body are interrelated, so too are the Five Elements interrelated. The four major types of relationships among the Five Elements are:

- generating
- controlling
- overcontrolling
- reverse controlling

The *generating* relationship can be understood as a mother-son relationship. The mother gives birth to the son and feeds the son. The mother generates and nourishes the son. There are five mother-son pairs within the Five Elements (see figure 10):

- Wood generates (is the mother of) Fire.
- Fire generates Earth.
- Earth generates Metal.
- Metal generates Water.
- Water generates Wood.

These relationships can be seen in the natural world, where wood ignites to start a fire, fire produces ash that falls to earth, earth can be mined for metal, metal carries water (as in a bucket or a pipe), and plants grow from spring rain.

Applying this to the organs of the body, a healthy mother organ nourishes the son organ. Therefore, a healthy liver (Wood element) with balanced soul, energy, and matter (positive shen qi jing) and without blockages (negative shen qi jing) will fully nourish the soul, energy, and matter of the heart (Fire element). In the same way, a healthy heart will nourish the spleen (Earth element); a healthy spleen will nourish the lungs (Metal element); healthy lungs will nourish the kidneys (Water element); and healthy kidneys will nourish the liver (Wood element).

The generating or mother-son relationships among the Five Elements are extremely important.

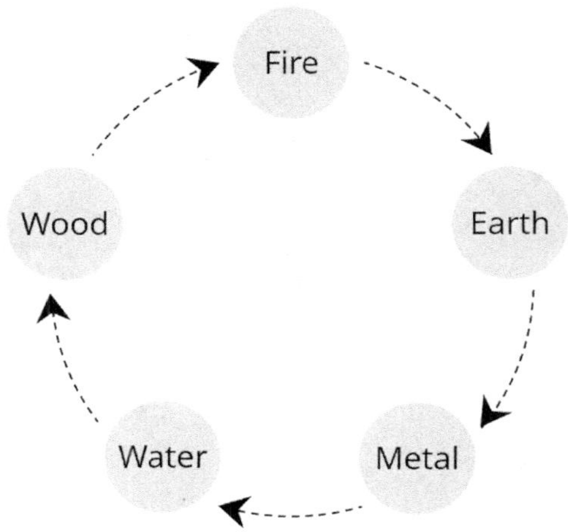

Figure 10. Generating relationships of the Five Elements

The *controlling* relationship shows the order of dominance or control among the Five Elements (see figure 11):

- Wood controls Earth.
- Earth controls Water.
- Water controls Fire.
- Fire controls Metal.
- Metal controls Wood.

In the natural world, wood draws nutrients from earth, earth dams water, water puts out fire, fire melts metal, and metal chops wood.

The *overcontrolling* and *reverse controlling* relationships are unbalanced relationships that can be used to describe and explain pathological conditions in the organs of the body. These relationships and conditions are caused by negative shen qi jing blockages.

Five Elements theory can be used to guide you to balance the physical body, emotional body, mental body, spiritual body, relationships, and finances. It can be applied to balance nature. It can help balance planets, stars, galaxies, and universes.

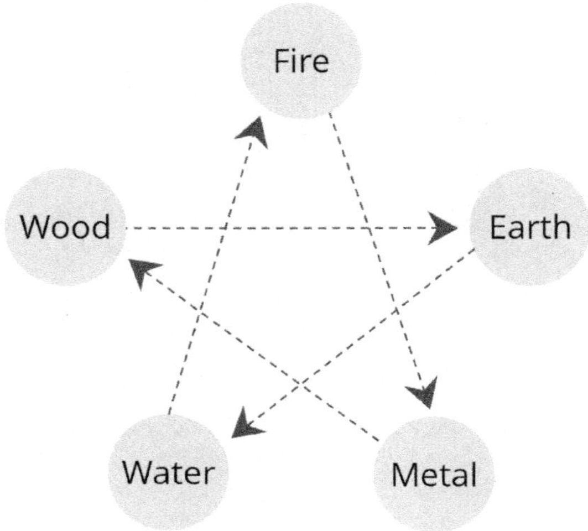

Figure 11. Controlling relationships of the Five Elements

Another major theory and core teaching of traditional Chinese medicine is named *zang fu* 臟腑. "Zang" means *viscera*. "Fu" means *bowels*. Zang fu includes five zang organs, six fu organs, and "extraordinary" organs.

The five zang organs are liver, heart, spleen, lungs, and kidneys. These are the yin organs of the Five Elements. Five of the six fu organs are the paired organs of the zang organs. They are the yang organs of the Five Elements. (See figure 8.) Therefore, the five zang-fu pairs are:

- Wood element: liver (zang), gallbladder (fu)
- Fire element: heart (zang), small intestine (fu)
- Earth element: spleen (zang), stomach (fu)
- Metal element: lungs (zang), large intestine (fu)
- Water element: kidneys (zang), urinary bladder (fu)

The sixth fu organ is the San Jiao 三焦. "San" means *three*. "Jiao" means *burnt*. The San Jiao or Triple Burner is the largest fu organ, although it is not an actual organ. Rather, it is the space in the body (three visceral cavities) that holds all of the internal organs.

The components of the San Jiao are the Upper Jiao, Middle Jiao, and Lower Jiao. The Upper Jiao is the area of the body above the diaphragm. It holds the heart and lungs. The Middle Jiao is the space in the body between the diaphragm and the level of the navel. It holds the pancreas, stomach, and spleen. The Lower Jiao is the space in the body from the level of the navel down to the bottom of the torso and the genitals. It holds the small and large intestines, urinary bladder, kidneys, reproductive organs, sexual organs, and liver. See figure 15 on page 90.

Although the liver is physically located in the Middle Jiao, traditional Chinese medicine believes that the liver and kidneys have the same source and a close relationship. Five Elements theory teaches that the kidney is the mother of the liver. Therefore, the liver is included in the Lower Jiao.

The "extraordinary" organs include the brain, bone marrow, bones, and uterus.

Why am I including this teaching of the Five Elements in this book? It is important to understand that to offer healing with the six sacred Tao power techniques for any one of the five major organs (yin organs or zang organs) will help heal everything associated with its element. The yin organ is the authority organ for its element, and so all of the organs, tissues, and fluids belonging to that element will receive healing benefits simultaneously. The emotional imbalances belonging to that element will also receive healing benefits simultaneously.

For example, the liver is the authority organ of the Wood element. The Wood element includes the gallbladder, eyes, tendons, and nails in the physical body and anger in the emotional body. When you offer healing for your liver, the other organs (gallbladder, eyes), tissues (tendons and nails), and emotional imbalance (anger) in the Wood element will also receive healing, prevention of sickness, and rejuvenation. The same is true for each of the five elements.

In my book, *Soul Healing Miracles*,[9] I explained Five Elements wisdom in detail. Here I will summarize the essence of Five Elements theory in traditional Chinese medicine.

Liver

- Stores and regulates blood
- Regulates and maintains the flows of qi and blood
  - Regulates emotions
  - Assists digestion and absorption of food
  - Maintains free flows of qi and blood
- Dominates and controls the tendons and manifests in the nails
- Opens into the eyes through the meridians; specifically, the eyes are connected to the liver meridian

Heart

- Governs blood and blood vessels
- Manifests on the face
- Houses the mind and takes charge of mental activities
- Opens into the tongue through the meridians
- Sweat is the fluid of the heart

Spleen

- Absorbs, transports, distributes, and transforms nutrients to nourish the whole body, from head to toe, skin to bone
  - Absorbs, distributes, and transforms nutrients
  - Transports and transforms liquids
- Controls and maintains blood flow within the blood vessels
- Dominates the muscles and four extremities
- Opens into the mouth through the meridians and manifests on the lips

---

[9] Dr. and Master Zhi Gang Sha, *Soul Healing Miracles: Ancient and New Sacred Wisdom, Knowledge, and Practical Techniques for Healing the Spiritual, Mental, Emotional, and Physical Bodies*, Dallas, TX/Toronto, ON: BenBella Books/Heaven's Library Publication Corp., 2013.

Lungs

- Dominate qi, including respiratory qi and whole-body qi
  - Control respiratory qi
  - Control whole-body qi
- Dominate, descend, and distribute qi, food essence, and body fluids to all systems, organs, and meridians, as well as to skin, hair, and muscles
- Regulate the water passages and help to maintain normal water metabolism
- Open into the nose through the meridians

Kidneys

- Store pre-natal and post-natal jing (matter) and dominate development and reproduction
  - Inherited essence of life (pre-natal jing)
  - Developed essence of life (post-natal jing)
- Dominate water metabolism
- Receive qi
- Dominate the bones, manufacture marrow to fill the brain, and manifest in the hair
- Open into the ears through the meridians and dominate anterior and posterior orifices

I would like to emphasize the wisdom of the relationships between the physical organs and emotions within the five elements. As we now know, human beings are composed of four interconnected and inseparable bodies: the physical, the emotional, the mental, and the spiritual. Imbalance and illness in any one body will influence and can cause sickness in the other bodies.

The connection between the physical body and the emotional body was recognized and released thousands of years ago by traditional Chinese medicine practitioners. From astute observations, ancient Chinese healers knew that liver illness in the physical body is linked with anger and rage in the emotional body. The converse is also true. They understood that unresolved anger in the emotional body could cause dysfunction of the liver, which could lead to other problems. In fact, ancient wisdom states anger is the most common cause of cancer.

Similar links were observed between other emotions and the physical organs and are still valid. People with heart problems are more prone to anxiety, depression, excitement, and joyful extremes in the emotional body. Conversely, long-term anxiety, depression, and too much excitement or happiness can give rise to heart problems. Spleen and stomach problems often result in worry, while worrying too much can generate spleen and stomach problems.

The interconnectedness of the emotional and physical bodies extends to the emotions of grief and fear. If you have lung illness, you are more susceptible to sadness and grief, and vice versa. Kidney problems are connected with fear in the emotional body. This can be seen when the involuntary release of urine is a common reaction to a sudden fright.

Let us look a bit more deeply into the connection between anger in the emotional body and the liver. People with a liver condition such as hepatitis, cirrhosis, or a tumor or cancer in the liver are generally easily upset. The converse is also true. If you are often angry and fly into rages at the slightest provocation, your constant anger hurts your liver by blocking its energy.

Think of the last time you argued so heatedly with a family member or a colleague—or a stranger—that you lost your temper. Regardless of what upset you, you probably also lost your appetite at that time. Everybody has had this experience. When you are upset, anger stimulates the liver cells and makes them overactive. As a result, more energy than usual radiates from the liver, putting pressure on the stomach, which causes you to lose your appetite. Loss of appetite is only one of the early symptoms of liver stress caused by anger. Other manifestations can include poor digestion, liver disease, and cancer.

Long-term anger like holding a perpetual grudge or regularly flying into a rage causes the liver to constantly radiate extra energy. If the surrounding tissues and organs cannot dissipate this excess energy quickly enough, an energy blockage will build up in and around the liver. Over time, the blockage will result in liver dysfunction, liver disease, or other complications such as cancer.

ꙮ ꙮ ꙮ

Five Elements is a universal law. The theory and practice of Five Elements apply to a human being. They apply to Mother Earth. They apply to countless planets, stars, galaxies, and universes.

Five Elements is one of the most important healing principles and wisdom in traditional Chinese medicine. The wisdom is profound and very deep. There is flexibility and creativity within the Five Elements. You, dear reader, can gain deeper wisdom and benefits by joining me in the next chapter to apply the Five Elements to heal and transform your life.

5

Apply Six Sacred Tao Power Techniques to Heal the Five Elements of the Physical Body and the Emotional Body

EVERY HUMAN BEING HAS five elements. Every animal has five elements. All of the countless planets, stars, galaxies, and universes have five elements. To balance the five elements is to heal and transform.

Since ancient times, three sacred techniques for healing and transformation have been commonly used in many cultures and traditions. In Chinese, they are called:

- shen mi 身密, which means *body secret*
- kou mi 口密, which means *mouth secret*
- yi mi 意密, which means *thinking secret*

In this book, shen mi is Body Power, kou mi is Sound Power, and yi mi is Mind Power. I have shared three additional sacred power techniques, which are Soul Power, Breath Power, and Tao Calligraphy Power.

I emphasize again that to apply any one of the six sacred power techniques is powerful. To apply the traditional three power techniques (Body Power, Sound Power, Mind Power) together is more powerful.

To apply all six of the sacred power Tao techniques together is extremely powerful.

You can practice for five to ten minutes per time. You can practice for thirty minutes, one hour, or longer. There is no time limit. The longer you practice, the more benefits you could receive. I wish you and every reader to apply and practice dedicatedly with all six sacred Tao power techniques together to heal and transform every aspect of your life, including health, relationships, finances, and more.

Let us apply the six sacred Tao power techniques together to heal and transform the five elements of the physical and emotional bodies.

Wood element

Apply the six sacred Tao power techniques to heal the Wood element, including the liver (the zang organ of the Wood element), gallbladder (the fu organ of the Wood element), eyes (the sense organ), tendons and nails (the body tissues), and anger (the unbalanced emotion).

Body Power. Place one palm over the liver. Place the other palm on the lower abdomen below the navel.

Soul Power. Say *hello* to inner souls:[10]

Dear soul heart mind body of my liver, gallbladder, eyes, tendons, nails, and the emotional body of the Wood element,
I love you, honor you, and appreciate you.
You have the power to heal and rejuvenate my liver, gallbladder, eyes, tendons, and nails and to heal and prevent anger.
Do a good job.
Thank you.

[10] Your inner souls are the souls of your own shen qi jing (soul, heart, mind, energy, matter). They include your "body soul" (your main soul), the souls of your systems, organs, tissues, and cells, the souls of the spaces and channels in your body, and more.

Say *hello* to outer souls:[11]

Dear Tao Source and Divine,
Dear buddhas, saints (you may name the heavenly beings or spiritual fathers and mothers you believe in),
Dear Heaven, Mother Earth, and countless planets, stars, galaxies, and universes,
I love you, honor you, and appreciate you.
Please forgive my ancestors and me for all the mistakes we have made in all lifetimes related to the liver, gallbladder, eyes, tendons, nails, and anger.
I am sincerely sorry for all these mistakes.
I apologize from the bottom of my heart to all the souls my ancestors and I have hurt or harmed in these ways.
In order to be forgiven, I will serve unconditionally.
To chant and meditate is to serve.
I will chant and meditate as much as I can.
I will offer unconditional service as much as I can.
I unconditionally forgive anyone who hurt or harmed me or my ancestors in all lifetimes.
I am extremely grateful.
Thank you.

Mind Power. Visualize golden light shining in and around the liver. This is the basic visualization you can always use to heal and transform the liver and the entire Wood element. When we move to Sound Power below, we will add more components to increase the power of the visualization.

Breath Power. When you inhale, allow your abdomen to expand. When you exhale, contract your abdomen. Be sure to inhale and exhale smoothly, evenly, and naturally. The duration and depth of each breath —inhalation and exhalation—depends on your personal condition. It would be different for different people. Follow nature's way. As you

---

[11] Outer souls are the countless souls outside of your own shen qi jing. Generally speaking, we say *hello* to Heaven's leaders (Tao Source and the Divine/God) and Heaven's saints (whomever you believe in), to Mother Earth, the sun, the moon, and to the countless planets, stars, galaxies, and universes.

continue to practice in this way, the duration and depth of your breaths will increase, little by little. I emphasize again the key principle is to *follow nature's way*. Remember never to prolong your breaths deliberately. Your breaths will get longer naturally through more practice.

Sound Power. As we chant, we combine the Sound Power with Breath Power and a more refined Mind Power visualization. For this and the other practices in this chapter, see the animations that have been created for you with my chanting.

Step 1

a. Inhale. Visualize golden light going from your nose down through the center of your body to the bottom of your torso, where it gathers as a ball in your first energy chakra[12] (first Soul House).

b. Exhale. Chant "Xu" (pronounced *shü*), the sacred sound for the Wood element. At the same time, visualize the golden light ball rotating up from the first Soul House to the liver, where it explodes and radiates in all directions from the liver.

c. Repeat steps 1a and 1b for a total of seven times.

Step 2

a. Inhale. Visualize golden light going from your nose down through the center of your body to the bottom of your torso, where it gathers as a ball in your first energy chakra (first Soul House).

b. Exhale. Chant "Xu Xu Xu." At the same time, visualize the golden light ball rotating up from the first Soul House to the liver, where it rotates, explodes, and radiates in all directions.

c. Repeat steps 2a and 2b for a total of four times.

---

[12] A fist sized space rests on the bottom of your torso. It is a spiritual energy center called the root chakra in ancient teachings of the Vedas and Hinduism. It is the first of seven major energy chakras that I teach are also the houses for one's body soul. You will learn about the power and significance of the chakras/Soul Houses in chapter eight, as well as their great importance for healing and transformation. See figure 14 on page 88.

Step 3

a. Inhale. Same visualization as in steps 1a and 2a.

b. Exhale. Chant:

Xu Ya (pronounced *shü yah*)
Xu Ya Xu Ya You (pronounced *shü yah shü yah yō*)
Xu Ya Xu Ya You
Xu Ya Xu Ya Xu Ya You
Xu Ya Xu Ya Xu Ya Xu Ya You

As you chant these five lines, inhale quickly after each line and visualize the golden light ball rotating as follows:

When you chant line 1, the golden light ball rotates up from the first energy chakra (Soul House) to the liver, then to the Kun Gong,[13] and back to the first Soul House.

When you chant lines 2 through 5, the golden light ball rotates up from the first energy chakra (Soul House) to the liver, then to the Kun Gong, and back down to the root chakra. When you chant "You" in these lines, visualize the golden light ball making a circle. It goes into the spinal cord through an invisible hole in front of the tailbone, then flows up the spinal cord to the occipital area, and then goes into and through the brain up to the crown chakra (seventh Soul House) atop your head. From there, it goes back down inside your nasal cavity to the palate, and then down through the fifth, fourth, third, and second chakras (Soul Houses) back to the root chakra (first Soul House). See figure 14 on page 88.

c. Repeat steps 3a and 3b for a total of four times.

---

[13] "Kun" is the name of one of the hexagrams in *Yi Jing* (*I Ching*). "Gong" means *temple*. The Kun Gong is a space in the body located behind the navel. The Kun Gong is very significant for qi, for enlightening the body, for the advanced spiritual journey, and much more. See my book, *Tao II: The Way of Healing, Rejuvenation, Longevity, and Immortality* (New York/Toronto: Atria Books/Heaven's Library Publication Corp., 2010) for more teachings about the Kun Gong. The Kun Gong is most important for daily life because it is the place that holds the "oil lamp" that sustains and fuels physical life.

You may chant aloud or silently. Doing both yang and yin chanting every time you practice is best.

Tao Calligraphy Power. Tao Calligraphy carries Tao shen qi jing, which is Tao Source soul, heart, mind, energy, and matter. This Tao Source information system of positive shen qi jing can transform negative shen qi jing of the Wood element and every aspect of life. I am including one Tao Calligraphy in this book specifically to support the healing and transformation of your Wood element.

Close. End your healing, blessing, rejuvenation, and transformation practice session by saying:

> *Hao. Hao. Hao.* (Mandarin Chinese for *good, perfect, healthy,* pronounced *how)*
> *Thank you. Thank you. Thank you.* (to all the souls who supported your practice)

The Tao Calligraphy *Xu* (figure 12) carries Tao Source positive shen qi jing to heal and transform the negative shen qi jing in the Wood element, including liver, gallbladder, eyes, tendons, nails, and healing and prevention of anger.

As I mentioned in chapter one, you can apply Tao Calligraphy in three major ways: trace, chant, write.

1. Trace Tao Calligraphy

There are sacred connections between the five fingers and the five elements through the energy channels.

The index finger connects with the Wood element, including the liver, gallbladder, eyes, tendons, nails, anger in the emotional body, and more.

The middle finger connects with the Fire element, including the heart, small intestine, blood vessels, tongue, depression and anxiety in the emotional body, and more.

The ring finger connects with the Metal element, including the lungs, large intestine, skin, nose, sadness and grief in the emotional body, and more.

The baby finger connects with the Water element, including the kidneys, urinary bladder, bones and joints, ears, fear in the emotional body, and more.

The thumb connects with the Earth element, including the spleen, stomach, muscles, mouth, lips, gums, teeth, worry in the emotional body, and more.

All of these connections are through the meridians. The meridians are the pathways of energy. Therefore, when you trace the Tao Source Calligraphy *Xu* with your fingertips (see figure 4 on page 7) or your Dan (see figure 6 on page 9), the Tao Source positive shen qi jing field will come to your Wood element for healing and transformation. See the tracing pathway for the Tao Calligraphy *Xu* shown in figure 13.

I emphasize again:

To trace Tao Calligraphy is to receive the positive shen qi jing within the Tao Calligraphy to heal and transform the negative shen qi jing in your body.

The positive shen qi jing carried by a Tao Calligraphy create a Tao Calligraphy healing field. To trace a Tao Calligraphy is to connect with its field. *What you trace is what you become.*

2. Chant the sacred sound of Tao Calligraphy

To chant the sacred sound is to embody the positive shen qi jing that the Tao Calligraphy carries. To chant a Tao Calligraphy is also to connect with its field. *What you chant is what you become.*

3. Write Tao Calligraphy

You can use a brush to write Tao Calligraphy or you can use any pen to write Tao Calligraphy. My trained and certified Tao Calligraphy Teachers and I offer a special training program to teach you how to use a brush to write a formal Yi Bi Zi calligraphy. To write Tao Calligraphy is one of the most powerful ways to connect with the Tao Calligraphy healing field. *What you write is what you become.*

Figure 12. Tao Calligraphy *Xu*, the sacred sound for the Wood element

Figure 13. Tracing pathway of Tao Calligraphy "Xu"

When you trace or write a Tao Calligraphy, tracing or writing becomes your Body Power. (We will focus on tracing.) It can be difficult to apply multiple sacred Tao power techniques simultaneously when you are applying Tao Calligraphy Power by tracing. Relax. Just do what you can do. For example, you can trace together only with chanting (Sound Power). You can trace and simply listen to my chanting on the videos that you have access to. (See page xi.) You can even apply *only* Tao Calligraphy Power by tracing after you have done the rest of the practice. Once you have done the Soul Power "say *hello*" invocation, any of the other sacred Tao power techniques in the practice will support the healing and transformation requested, whether applied alone or in any combination.

Yin-yang pair alternating practice

I would like to share another secret about applying the six sacred Tao power techniques. We live in the yin-yang world. We live between Heaven and Mother Earth. Heaven belongs to yang. Mother Earth belongs to yin.

For Heaven, Mother Earth, and human being, yin yang is the number one spiritual law and principle. Everyone and everything can be divided into yin yang aspects. The six sacred Tao power techniques are divided into yin yang aspects.

Placing one palm over the liver and placing the other palm on the lower abdomen are a yin-yang pair within Body Power.

Chanting *xu* aloud and chanting *xu* silently form a yin-yang pair within Sound Power.

Focusing your mind on the liver and focusing on the whole body are a yin-yang pair within Mind Power.

Invoking outer souls (Tao Source, nature, countless planets, stars, galaxies, and universes, Divine, Heaven, all kinds of saints, and buddhas) and invoking inner souls (your own shen qi jing of the body, systems, organs, cells, spaces) to bless your liver and body are a yin-yang pair within Soul Power.

Inhaling and exhaling are a yin-yang pair within Breath Power.

Chanting and tracing the Tao Calligraphy *Xu* to bless, heal, and rejuvenate your liver are a yin-yang pair within Tao Calligraphy Power.

Why is the yin-yang pair alternating practice sacred and vital? It can be summarized in one sentence:

Yin-yang pair alternating practice is to balance yin and yang and to join yin and yang as one in order to heal and transform.

Yin Yang is a universal law. To join yin and yang as one could offer the highest healing and transformation.

How to find other Tao Calligraphies in order to apply Tao Calligraphy Power

I am including the Tao Calligraphy *Xu* in this book as a gift. As you have learned, Xu is the sacred sound to heal and transform the Wood element, so this Tao Calligraphy is primarily to serve your Wood element.

How then can you apply Tao Calligraphy Power in the practices in the rest of this chapter (for the other four elements) and indeed in the rest of this book (for the mental body, spiritual body, seven energy chakras, relationships, finances, and more)?

Every one of my books published since 2013 includes at least one Tao Calligraphy. I recommend you use the Tao Calligraphy *Da Ai* (greatest love) in my eponymous 2017 book[14] or the Tao Calligraphy *Da Kuan Shu* (greatest forgiveness) in my eponymous 2019 book.[15] These books have many other practices that can benefit you and they are pocket-sized, so are easy to carry with you.

You can also purchase laminated cards (4 x 6 in. or smaller) of several of my Tao Calligraphies, including all Ten Da natures of Tao and *Xiang Ai Ping An He Xie* (Love Peace Harmony).

If you cannot use the above options, you can trace the reproduction of the Tao Calligraphy *Da Ai* on the back cover of this book.

The best way to practice is to practice in one of my Master Sha Tao Centers. They have the most powerful Tao Calligraphy healing fields created by thirty to more than one hundred of my original Tao Calligraphies, including all kinds of organs, parts of the body, bodily tissues, emotional

---

[14] Dr. and Master Zhi Gang Sha, Master Maya Mackie, and Master Francisco Quintero, *Greatest Love: Unblock Your Life in 30 Minutes a Day with the Power of Unconditional Love*, Dallas, TX/Richmond Hill, ON: BenBella Books/Heaven's Library Publication Corp., 2017.

[15] Dr. and Master Zhi Gang Sha, Master Cynthia Deveraux, and Master David Lusch, *Greatest Forgiveness: Bring Joy and Peace to Your Life with the Power of Unconditional Forgiveness*, Dallas, TX/Richmond Hill, ON: BenBella Books/Heaven's Library Publication Corp., 2019.

imbalances, Ten Da qualities, energy centers, other important spaces in the body, and more. As of early 2020, I have created ten such Centers worldwide. They are in:

- Toronto, Ontario
- Honolulu, Hawaii
- San Francisco, California
- Vancouver, British Columbia
- London, England
- Amersfoort, the Netherlands
- Antwerp, Belgium
- Sydney, Australia
- Bordeaux, France
- Martinique

Join any session led by one of my Tao Chang Grandmaster or Master Healers and Teachers to access the highest and most positive information systems of the Tao Calligraphy healing fields. Many classes and practice sessions are available remotely by live webcast, so you can find sessions that are convenient for you.

Fire element

Apply the six sacred power techniques to heal the Fire element, including the heart (the zang organ of the Fire element), small intestine (the fu organ of the Fire element), tongue (the sense organ), blood vessels (the body tissue), and depression and anxiety (the unbalanced emotions).

Body Power. Place one palm over the heart. Place the other palm on the lower abdomen below the navel.

Soul Power. Say *hello* to inner souls:

Dear soul heart mind body of my heart, small intestine, tongue, blood vessels, and the emotional body of the Fire element,
I love you, honor you, and appreciate you.

You have the power to heal and rejuvenate my heart, small intestine, tongue, and blood vessels and to heal and prevent depression and anxiety.
Do a good job.
Thank you.

Say *hello* to outer souls:

Dear Tao Source and Divine,
Dear buddhas, saints (name the heavenly beings or spiritual fathers and mothers you believe in),
Dear Heaven, Mother Earth, and countless planets, stars, galaxies, and universes,
I love you, honor you, and appreciate you.
Please forgive my ancestors and me for all the mistakes we have made in all lifetimes related to the heart, small intestine, tongue, blood vessels, depression, and anxiety.
I am sincerely sorry for all these mistakes.
I apologize from the bottom of my heart to all the souls my ancestors and I have hurt or harmed in these ways.
In order to be forgiven, I will serve unconditionally.
To chant and meditate is to serve.
I will chant and meditate as much as I can.
I will offer unconditional service as much as I can.
I unconditionally forgive anyone who hurt or harmed me or my ancestors in all lifetimes.
I am extremely grateful.
Thank you.

Mind Power. Visualize golden light shining in and around the heart.

Breath Power. Inhale and expand your abdomen. Exhale and contract your abdomen. Inhale and exhale smoothly, evenly, and naturally. Remember that the length of each inhalation and exhalation depends on your personal condition.

Sound Power. As we chant, we combine the Sound Power with Breath Power and a more refined Mind Power visualization.

Step 1

a. Inhale. Visualize golden light going from your nose down through the center of your body to the bottom of your torso, where it gathers as a ball in your first energy chakra (first Soul House).

b. Exhale. Chant "Ah," the sacred sound for the Fire element. At the same time, visualize the golden light ball rotating up from the first Soul House to the heart, where it explodes and radiates in all directions from the heart.

c. Repeat steps 1a and 1b for a total of seven times.

Step 2

a. Inhale. Visualize golden light going from your nose down through the center of your body to the bottom of your torso, where it gathers as a ball in your first energy chakra (first Soul House).

b. Exhale. Chant "Ah Ah Ah." At the same time, visualize the golden light ball rotating up from the first Soul House to the heart, where it rotates, explodes, and radiates in all directions.

c. Repeat steps 2a and 2b for a total of four times.

Step 3

a. Inhale. Same visualization as in steps 1a and 2a.

b. Exhale. Chant:

Ah Ya (pronounced *ah yah*)
Ah Ya Ah Ya You (pronounced *ah yah ah yah yō*)
Ah Ya Ah Ya You
Ah Ya Ah Ya Ah Ya You
Ah Ya Ah Ya Ah Ya Ah Ya You

As you chant these five lines, inhale quickly after each line and visualize the golden light ball rotating as follows:

When you chant line 1, the golden light ball rotates up from the first chakra (Soul House) to the heart, then to the Kun Gong, and back down to the root chakra (first Soul House).

When you chant lines 2 through 5, the golden light ball rotates up from the first energy chakra (Soul House) to the heart, then to the Kun Gong, and back down to the first Soul House. When you chant "You" in these lines, visualize the golden ball making a circle. It goes into the spinal cord through an invisible hole in front of the tailbone, then flows up the spinal cord to the occipital area, and then goes into and through the brain up to the crown chakra (seventh Soul House) atop your head. From there, it goes back down inside your nasal cavity to the palate, and then down through the fifth, fourth, third, and second chakras (Soul Houses) back to the root chakra (first Soul House). See figure 14 on page 88.

c. Repeat steps 3a and 3b for a total of four times.

You may chant aloud or silently. Doing both yang and yin chanting every time you practice is best.

Tao Calligraphy Power. Trace *Da Ai*, greatest love, or *Da Kuan Shu*, greatest forgiveness. (See "How to find other Tao Calligraphies in order to apply Tao Calligraphy Power" on page 59 above.)

When you trace, tracing becomes your Body Power. Do not worry about trying to apply several other sacred Tao power techniques simultaneously while you are tracing. Relax and just do what comes naturally and with ease to you. Once you have done the Soul Power "say *hello*" invocation, any of the other sacred Tao power techniques in the practice will support the healing and transformation requested, whether applied alone or in any combination.

Close. End your practice session by saying:

Hao. Hao. Hao.
Thank you. Thank you. Thank you.

Earth element

Apply the six sacred power techniques to heal the Earth element, including the spleen (the zang organ of the Earth element), stomach (the fu organ of the Earth element), mouth, lips, teeth, and gums (the sense organ), muscles (the body tissue), and worry (the unbalanced emotion).

Body Power. Place one palm over the spleen. Place the other palm on the lower abdomen below the navel.

Soul Power. Say *hello* to inner souls:

Dear soul heart mind body of my spleen, stomach, mouth, lips, teeth, gums, muscles, and the emotional body of the Earth element,
I love you, honor you, and appreciate you.
You have the power to heal and rejuvenate my spleen, stomach, mouth, lips, teeth, gums, and muscles and to heal and prevent worry.
Do a good job.
Thank you.

Say *hello* to outer souls:

Dear Tao Source and Divine,
Dear buddhas, saints (name the heavenly beings or spiritual fathers and mothers you believe in),
Dear Heaven, Mother Earth, and countless planets, stars, galaxies, and universes,
I love you, honor you, and appreciate you.
Please forgive my ancestors and me for all the mistakes we have made in all lifetimes related to the spleen, stomach, mouth, lips, teeth, gums, muscles, and worry.
I am sincerely sorry for all these mistakes.
I apologize from the bottom of my heart to all the souls my ancestors and I have hurt or harmed in these ways.
In order to be forgiven, I will serve unconditionally.
To chant and meditate is to serve.
I will chant and meditate as much as I can.
I will offer unconditional service as much as I can.
I unconditionally forgive anyone who hurt or harmed me or my ancestors in all lifetimes.
I am extremely grateful.
Thank you.

Mind Power. Visualize golden light shining in and around the spleen.

Breath Power. Inhale and expand your abdomen. Exhale and contract your abdomen. Make sure you inhale and exhale smoothly, evenly, and naturally. Remember that the length of each inhalation and exhalation depends on your personal condition.

Sound Power. As we chant, we combine the Sound Power with Breath Power and a more refined Mind Power visualization.

Step 1

a. Inhale. Visualize golden light going from your nose down through the center of your body to the bottom of your torso, where it gathers as a ball in your first energy chakra (first Soul House).
b. Exhale. Chant "Hu" (pronounced *hoo*), the sacred sound for the Earth element. At the same time, visualize the golden light ball rotating up from the first Soul House to the spleen, where it explodes and radiates in all directions from the spleen.
c. Repeat steps 1a and 1b for a total of seven times.

Step 2

a. Inhale. Visualize golden light going from your nose down through the center of your body to the bottom of your torso, where it gathers as a ball in your first energy chakra (first Soul House).
b. Exhale. Chant "Hu Hu Hu." At the same time, visualize the golden light ball rotating up from the first Soul House to the spleen, where it rotates, explodes, and radiates in all directions.
c. Repeat steps 2a and 2b for a total of four times.

Step 3

a. Inhale. Same visualization as in steps 1a and 2a.
b. Exhale. Chant:

   Hu Ya (pronounced *hoo yah*)
   Hu Ya Hu Ya You (pronounced *hoo yah hoo yah yō*)
   Hu Ya Hu Ya You

Hu Ya Hu Ya Hu Ya You
Hu Ya Hu Ya Hu Ya Hu Ya You

As you chant these five lines, inhale quickly after each line and visualize the golden light ball rotating as follows:

When you chant line 1, the golden light ball rotates up from the first chakra (Soul House) to the spleen, then to the Kun Gong, and back down to the root chakra (first Soul House).

When you chant lines 2 through 5, the golden light ball rotates up from the first energy chakra (Soul House) to the spleen, then to the Kun Gong, and back down to the first Soul House. When you chant "You" in these lines, visualize the golden ball making a circle. It goes into the spinal cord through an invisible hole in front of the tailbone, then flows up the spinal cord to the occipital area, and then goes into and through the brain up to the crown chakra (seventh Soul House) atop your head. From there, it goes back down inside your nasal cavity to the palate, and then down through the fifth, fourth, third, and second chakras (Soul Houses) back to the root chakra (first Soul House). See figure 14 on page 88.

c. Repeat steps 3a and 3b for a total of four times.

You may chant aloud or silently. Doing both yang and yin chanting every time you practice is best.

Tao Calligraphy Power. Trace *Da Ai*, greatest love, or *Da Kuan Shu*, greatest forgiveness. (See "How to find other Tao Calligraphies in order to apply Tao Calligraphy Power" on page 59 above.)

When you trace, tracing becomes your Body Power. You may combine tracing with Mind Power, Sound Power, and/or Breath Power if you wish, or you may simply focus on tracing.

Close. End your practice session by saying:

Hao. Hao. Hao.
Thank you. Thank you. Thank you.

Metal element

Apply the six sacred Tao power techniques to heal the Metal element, including the lungs (the zang organ of the Metal element), large intestine (the fu organ of the Metal element), nose (the sense organ), skin (the body tissue), and sadness and grief (the unbalanced emotions).

Body Power. Place one palm over a lung. Place the other palm on the lower abdomen below the navel. You may alternate hands and lungs during the practice.

Soul Power. Say *hello* to inner souls:

Dear soul heart mind body of my lungs, large intestine, nose, skin, and the emotional body of the Metal element,
I love you, honor you, and appreciate you.
You have the power to heal and rejuvenate my lungs, large intestine, nose, and skin and to heal and prevent sadness and grief.
Do a good job.
Thank you.

Say *hello* to outer souls:

Dear Tao Source and Divine,
Dear buddhas, saints (name the heavenly beings or spiritual fathers and mothers you believe in),
Dear Heaven, Mother Earth, and countless planets, stars, galaxies, and universes,
I love you, honor you, and appreciate you.
Please forgive my ancestors and me for all the mistakes we have made in all lifetimes related to the lungs, large intestine, nose, skin, sadness, and grief.
I am sincerely sorry for all these mistakes.
I apologize from the bottom of my heart to all the souls my ancestors and I have hurt or harmed in these ways.
In order to be forgiven, I will serve unconditionally.
To chant and meditate is to serve.
I will chant and meditate as much as I can.

I will offer unconditional service as much as I can.
I unconditionally forgive anyone who hurt or harmed me or my ancestors in all lifetimes.
I am extremely grateful.
Thank you.

Mind Power. Visualize golden light shining in and around the lungs.

Breath Power. Inhale and expand your abdomen. Exhale and contract your abdomen. Make sure you inhale and exhale smoothly, evenly, and naturally. Remember that the length of each inhalation and exhalation depends on your personal condition.

Sound Power. As we chant, we combine the Sound Power with Breath Power and a more refined Mind Power visualization.

Step 1

a. Inhale. Visualize golden light going from your nose down through the center of your body to the bottom of your torso, where it gathers as a ball in your first energy chakra (first Soul House).

b. Exhale. Chant "Si" (pronounced *sz*), the sacred sound for the Metal element. At the same time, visualize the golden light ball rotating up from the first Soul House to the lungs, where it explodes and radiates in all directions from the lungs.

c. Repeat steps 1a and 1b for a total of seven times.

Step 2

a. Inhale. Visualize golden light going from your nose down through the center of your body to the bottom of your torso, where it gathers as a ball in your first energy chakra (first Soul House).

b. Exhale. Chant "Si Si Si." At the same time, visualize the golden light ball rotating up from the first Soul House to the lungs, where it rotates, explodes, and radiates in all directions.

c. Repeat steps 2a and 2b for a total of four times.

Step 3

a. Inhale. Same visualization as in steps 1a and 2a.

b. Exhale. Chant:

   Si Ya (pronounced *sz yah*)
   Si Ya Si Ya You (pronounced *sz yah sz yah yō*)
   Si Ya Si Ya You
   Si Ya Si Ya Si Ya You
   Si Ya Si Ya Si Ya Si Ya You

   As you chant these five lines, inhale quickly after each line and visualize the golden light ball rotating as follows:

   When you chant line 1, the golden light ball rotates up from the first chakra (Soul House) to the lungs, then to the Kun Gong, and back down to the root chakra (first Soul House).

   When you chant lines 2 through 5, the golden light ball rotates up from the first energy chakra (Soul House) to the lungs, then to the Kun Gong, and back down to the first Soul House. When you chant "You" in these lines, visualize the golden ball making a circle. It goes into the spinal cord through an invisible hole in front of the tailbone, then flows up the spinal cord to the occipital area, and then goes into and through the brain up to the crown chakra (seventh Soul House) atop your head. From there, it goes back down inside your nasal cavity to the palate, and then down through the fifth, fourth, third, and second chakras (Soul Houses) back to the root chakra (first Soul House). See figure 14 on page 88.

c. Repeat steps 3a and 3b for a total of four times.

You may chant aloud or silently. Doing both yang and yin chanting every time you practice is best.

Tao Calligraphy Power. Trace *Da Ai,* greatest love, or *Da Kuan Shu,* greatest forgiveness. (See "How to find other Tao Calligraphies in order to apply Tao Calligraphy Power" on page 59 above.)

When you trace, tracing becomes your Body Power. You may combine tracing with Mind Power, Sound Power, and/or Breath Power if you wish, or you may simply focus on tracing.

Close. End your practice session by saying:

Hao. Hao. Hao.
Thank you. Thank you. Thank you.

Water element

Apply the six sacred Tao power techniques to heal the Water element, including the kidneys (the zang organ of the Water element), urinary bladder (the fu organ of the Water element), ears (the sense organ), bones and joints (the body tissue), and fear (the unbalanced emotion).

Body Power. Place one palm over a kidney. Place the other palm on the lower abdomen below the navel. If your hands or arms get tired, or even if not, you may alternate hands and kidneys during the practice.

Soul Power. Say *hello* to inner souls:

Dear soul heart mind body of my kidneys, urinary bladder, ears, bones, and the emotional body of the Water element,
I love you, honor you, and appreciate you.
You have the power to heal and rejuvenate my kidneys, urinary bladder, ears, bones, and joints and to heal and prevent fear.
Do a good job.
Thank you.

Say *hello* to outer souls:

Dear Tao Source and Divine,
Dear buddhas, saints (name the heavenly beings or spiritual fathers and mothers you believe in),
Dear Heaven, Mother Earth, and countless planets, stars, galaxies, and universes,
I love you, honor you, and appreciate you.

Please forgive my ancestors and me for all the mistakes we have made in all lifetimes related to the kidneys, urinary bladder, ears, bones, joints, and fear.
I am sincerely sorry for all these mistakes.
I apologize from the bottom of my heart to all the souls my ancestors and I have hurt or harmed in these ways.
In order to be forgiven, I will serve unconditionally.
To chant and meditate is to serve.
I will chant and meditate as much as I can.
I will offer unconditional service as much as I can.
I unconditionally forgive anyone who hurt or harmed me or my ancestors in all lifetimes.
I am extremely grateful.
Thank you.

Mind Power. Visualize golden light shining in and around the kidneys.

Breath Power. Inhale and expand your abdomen. Exhale and contract your abdomen. Make sure you inhale and exhale smoothly, evenly, and naturally. Remember that the length of each inhalation and exhalation depends on your personal condition.

Sound Power. As we chant, we combine the Sound Power with Breath Power and a more refined Mind Power visualization.

Step 1

a. Inhale. Visualize golden light going from your nose down through the center of your body to the bottom of your torso, where it gathers as a ball in your first energy chakra (first Soul House).

b. Exhale. Chant "Chui" (pronounced *chway*), the sacred sound for the Water element. At the same time, visualize the golden light ball rotating up from the first Soul House to the kidneys, where it explodes and radiates in all directions from the kidneys.

c. Repeat steps 1a and 1b for a total of seven times.

Step 2

a. Inhale. Visualize golden light going from your nose down through the center of your body to the bottom of your torso, where it gathers as a ball in your first energy chakra (first Soul House).

b. Exhale. Chant "Chui Chui Chui." At the same time, visualize the golden light ball rotating up from the first Soul House to the kidneys, where it rotates, explodes, and radiates in all directions.

c. Repeat steps 2a and 2b for a total of four times.

Step 3

a. Inhale. Same visualization as in steps 1a and 2a.

b. Exhale. Chant:

Chui Ya (pronounced *chway yah*)
Chui Ya Chui Ya You (pronounced *chway yah chway yah yō*)
Chui Ya Chui Ya You
Chui Ya Chui Ya Chui Ya You
Chui Ya Chui Ya Chui Ya Chui Ya You

As you chant these five lines, inhale quickly after each line and visualize the golden light ball rotating as follows:

When you chant line 1, the golden light ball rotates up from the first chakra (Soul House) to the kidneys, then to the Kun Gong, and back down to the root chakra (first Soul House).

When you chant lines 2 through 5, the golden light ball rotates up from the first energy chakra (Soul House) to the kidneys, then to the Kun Gong, and back down to the first Soul House. When you chant "You" in these lines, visualize the golden ball making a circle. It goes into the spinal cord through an invisible hole in front of the tailbone, then flows up the spinal cord to the occipital area, and then goes into and through the brain up to the crown chakra (seventh Soul House) atop your head. From there, it goes back down inside your nasal cavity to the palate, and then down through the fifth, fourth, third, and second chakras (Soul Houses) back to the root chakra (first Soul House). See figure 14 on page 88.

c. Repeat steps 3a and 3b for a total of four times.

You may chant aloud or silently. Doing both yang and yin chanting every time you practice is best.

Tao Calligraphy Power. Trace *Da Ai,* greatest love, or *Da Kuan Shu,* greatest forgiveness. (See "How to find other Tao Calligraphies in order to apply Tao Calligraphy Power" on page 59 above.)

When you trace, tracing becomes your Body Power. You may combine tracing with Mind Power, Sound Power, and/or Breath Power if you wish, or you may simply focus on tracing.

Close. End your practice session by saying:

> *Hao. Hao. Hao.*
> *Thank you. Thank you. Thank you.*

ജ ഉ ജ

To heal and transform the Five Elements is one of the most important and key practices for health, relationships, and finances. In this chapter, we have applied six sacred Tao power techniques to heal and transform the physical and emotional bodies. Let us next apply six sacred Tao power techniques to heal the mental body.

6

Apply Six Sacred Tao Power Techniques to Heal the Mental Body

THE MENTAL BODY IS the mind of a human being, of an animal, of anything and everything. Mind is consciousness. Everyone and everything is made of shen qi jing. In other words, everyone and everything has a soul, heart (spiritual core), mind (consciousness), and body (energy and matter). Blockages in the mind or consciousness are major blockages related to every aspect of life.

I emphasize again that some of the most important mind blockages, which are negative information or messages in the mind, are negative mindsets, negative attitudes, negative beliefs, ego, attachments, and more.

Numerous mental conditions also need healing and transformation. They include mental confusion, poor concentration, loss of memory, attention deficit disorder, eating disorders, obsessive-compulsive disorder, Alzheimer's disease, bipolar disorder, other serious mental disorders, and more.

I will share another important secret: in order to heal and balance the mental body, the key is the heart chakra or fourth Soul House, which I also call the Message Center.

The Message Center is one of the most important spiritual and energy centers in a human being. It is the center for soul healing and soul communication. The Message Center and the heart lead the consciousness. To heal and transform the Message Center is to transform the consciousness, including emotions, negative mindsets, negative attitudes, negative beliefs, ego, attachments, and all other kinds of mental blockages and challenges.

Let us apply six sacred Tao power techniques to heal and transform the mental body by healing and transforming the Message Center.

We will practice with the fourth of the Ten Da natures of Tao, Da Guang Ming, greatest light, to heal and transform the mental body. I emphasize the power and significance of Da Guang Ming as told in the sacred four-line Tao Source mantra of Da Guang Ming in chapter two:

The fourth of the Ten Da natures of Tao is greatest light and transparency.
I am inside Tao Source light.
Tao Source light is inside me.
The whole body is completely light and transparent.

Body Power. Place one palm over the Message Center (heart chakra, fourth Soul House), which is in the middle of your chest beside the heart. See figure 14 on page 88. Place the other palm over the brain.

Soul Power. Say *hello* to inner souls:

> *Dear soul heart mind body of my Message Center,*
> *Dear soul heart mind body of my mind,*
> *I love you, honor you, and appreciate you.*
> *You have the power to heal and transform my heart and my mind.*
> *Do a good job.*
> *Thank you.*

Say *hello* to outer souls:

> *Dear Tao Source and Divine,*
> *Dear buddhas, saints* (name the saints you believe in),

Dear Heaven, Mother Earth, and countless planets, stars, galaxies, and universes,
I love you, honor you, and appreciate you.
Please forgive my ancestors and me for all the mistakes we have made in all lifetimes related to the mind or mental body.
I am sincerely sorry for all these mistakes.
I apologize from the bottom of my heart to all the souls my ancestors and I have hurt or harmed by causing mind blockages or mental conditions.
In order to be forgiven, I will serve unconditionally.
To chant and meditate is to serve.
I will chant and meditate as much as I can.
I will offer unconditional service as much as I can.
I unconditionally forgive anyone who hurt or harmed my ancestors or me in all lifetimes.
I am extremely grateful.
Thank you.

Mind Power. Visualize golden light shining in and around the Message Center and the brain.

Breath Power. Inhale and expand your abdomen. Exhale and contract your abdomen. Make sure you inhale and exhale smoothly, evenly and naturally. Remember that the length of each inhalation and exhalation depends on your personal condition. Follow nature's way.

Sound Power. As we chant, we combine the Sound Power with Breath Power and a more refined Mind Power visualization. See the video with my chanting that has been created for you for this practice and all the major practices in this book.

Step 1

a. Inhale. Visualize golden light going from your nose down through the center of your body to the bottom of your torso, where it gathers as a ball in your first energy chakra (first Soul House).
b. Exhale. Chant "Guang Ming" (pronounced *gwahng ming*). At the same time, visualize the golden light ball rotating up from the first

Soul House to the Message Center, where it explodes and radiates in all directions from the Message Center.

c. Repeat steps 1a and 1b for a total of seven times.

Step 2

a. Inhale. Visualize golden light going from your nose down through the center of your body to the bottom of your torso, where it gathers as a ball in your first energy chakra (first Soul House).

b. Exhale. Chant "Guang Ming Guang Ming Guang Ming." At the same time, visualize the golden light ball rotating up from the first Soul House to the Message Center, where it rotates, explodes, and radiates in all directions.

c. Repeat steps 2a and 2b for a total of four times.

Step 3

a. Inhale. Same visualization as in steps 1a and 2a.

b. Exhale. Chant:

Guang Ming (pronounced *gwahng ming*)
Guang Ming Guang Ming Guang Ming
Guang Ming Guang Ming Guang Ming
Guang Ming Guang Ming Guang Ming
Guang Ming Guang Ming Guang Ming Guang Ming

As you chant these five lines, inhale quickly after each line and visualize the golden light ball rotating as follows:

When you chant line 1, the golden light ball rotates up from the first Soul House to the Message Center, then down through the Kun Gong, and back to the first Soul House.

When you chant lines 2 through 5, the golden light ball rotates up from the first Soul House to the Message Center, then down through the Kun Gong, and back to the first Soul House. Then, the golden ball makes a circle. It goes from the first Soul House into the spinal cord through an invisible hole in front of the tailbone, then flows up the spinal cord to the occipital area, and then goes into and through the brain up to the crown chakra (seventh Soul House) atop your head. From there, it goes back down inside your nasal cavity to the palate, and then down through the fifth, fourth, third, and second chakras (Soul Houses) back to the root chakra (first Soul House). See figure 14 on page 88.

c. Repeat steps 3a and 3b for a total of four times.

You may chant aloud or silently. Doing both yang and yin chanting every time you practice is best.

Tao Calligraphy Power. Trace *Da Ai,* greatest love, or *Da Kuan Shu,* greatest forgiveness. (See "How to find other Tao Calligraphies in order to apply Tao Calligraphy Power" on page 59 above.)

When you trace, tracing becomes your Body Power. You may combine tracing with Mind Power, Sound Power, and/or Breath Power if you wish, or you may simply focus on tracing.

Close. End your practice session by saying:

Hao. Hao. Hao.
Thank you. Thank you. Thank you.

ꕥ ꕥ ꕥ

We have applied six sacred Tao power techniques to heal and transform the mental body through Da Guang Ming, greatest light. Da Guang Ming is the fourth of the Ten Da. You can apply any of the other nine of the Ten Da qualities in the same way for transforming the mental body.

There are many unhealthy conditions of the mind or consciousness. The sacred wisdom and techniques that I have shared in this chapter can be applied to heal and transform all of them.

Practice. Practice. Practice.

Experience the transformation.

7

Apply Six Sacred Tao Power Techniques to Heal the Spiritual Body

A HUMAN BEING HAS countless souls. A human being has a body soul, souls of all systems, organs, cells, cell units, DNA, RNA, spaces between the cells, tiny matter inside the cells, and more.

Souls reincarnate lifetime after lifetime. Souls carry the wisdom, knowledge, and life experience memories of all lifetimes. Souls also carry the blockages of all lifetimes. Applying the six sacred Tao power techniques for healing the spiritual body is the key for healing all sickness.

Why? Soul is the boss. Recall the four sacred phrases in the Law of Shen Qi Jing:

靈到心到	ling dao xin dao	Soul arrives, heart follows.
心到意到	xin dao yi dao	Heart arrives, mind follows.
意到氣到	yi dao qi dao	Mind arrives, energy follows.
氣到血到	qi dao xue dao	Energy arrives, matter follows.

Our beloved soul is the warehouse of all information, the content of all messages from our physical body, emotional body, mental body, spiritual body, relationships, finances, and more in all lifetimes. Negative information or messages in the soul, which are the blockages of all lifetimes, are passed to the heart, mind, and body. The results can be all kinds of blockages, challenges, and negativities in the heart, mind, and body. Therefore, the importance of healing the spiritual body cannot be explained enough by words.

Heal and transform the soul first; then healing and transformation of every aspect of life will follow.

This sacred key for healing can be expressed in another way:

Heal and transform the spiritual body first; then healing and transformation of the mental, emotional, and physical bodies will follow.

Apply the six sacred Tao power techniques to heal and transform the spiritual body. In chapter two, I shared the ten greatest natures of Tao Source, Heaven, Mother Earth, and a human being.

Let us practice Da Ai, greatest love, to heal and transform the spiritual body. I emphasize the power and significance of Da Ai through the four-line sacred mantra I shared in chapter two:

First give greatest love, the first of the Ten Da natures of Tao.
Unconditional love
Melts all blockages.
Heart clear; soul, heart, and mind enlightened.

Body Power. Place one palm over your heart. Ancient wisdom teaches that the heart houses the mind and soul. Place your other palm on your lower abdomen below the navel.

Soul Power. Say *hello* to inner souls:

> *Dear soul heart mind body of my spiritual body,*
> *I love you, honor you, and appreciate you.*
> *You have the power to heal and transform yourselves.*
> *Do a good job.*
> *Thank you.*

Say *hello* to outer souls:

Dear Tao Source and Divine,
Dear buddhas, saints (name the saints you believe in),
Dear Heaven, Mother Earth, and countless planets, stars, galaxies, and universes,
I love you, honor you, and appreciate you.
Please forgive my ancestors and me for all the mistakes we have made in all lifetimes related to the spiritual journey and the spiritual body.
I am sincerely sorry for all these mistakes.
I apologize from the bottom of my heart to all the souls my ancestors and I have hurt or harmed by causing blockages to their spiritual journey or spiritual body.
In order to be forgiven, I will serve unconditionally.
To chant and meditate is to serve.
I will chant and meditate as much as I can.
I will offer unconditional service as much as I can.
I unconditionally forgive anyone who hurt or harmed my ancestors or me in all lifetimes.
I am extremely grateful.
Thank you.

Mind Power. Visualize golden light shining in and around the heart and throughout the entire body.

Breath Power. Inhale and let your abdomen expand. Exhale and contract your abdomen. Make sure you inhale and exhale smoothly, evenly, and naturally. Remember that the length of each inhalation and exhalation depends on your personal condition.

Sound Power. As we chant, we combine the Sound Power with Breath Power and a more refined Mind Power visualization. See the video with my chanting that has been created for you for this practice and all the major practices in this book.

Step 1

a. Inhale. Visualize golden light going from your nose down through the center of your body to the bottom of your torso, where it gathers as a ball in your first energy chakra (first Soul House).

b. Exhale. Chant "Da Ai" (pronounced *dah eye*). At the same time, visualize the golden light ball rotating up from the first Soul House to the heart, where it explodes and radiates in all directions from the heart.

c. Repeat steps 1a and 1b for a total of seven times.

Step 2

a. Inhale. Visualize golden light going from your nose down through the center of your body to the bottom of your torso, where it gathers as a ball in your first energy chakra (first Soul House).

b. Exhale. Chant "Da Ai Da Ai Da Ai." At the same time, visualize the golden light ball rotating up from the first Soul House to the heart, where it rotates, explodes, and radiates in all directions.

c. Repeat steps 2a and 2b for a total of four times.

Step 3

a. Inhale. Same visualization as in steps 1a and 2a.

b. Exhale. Chant:

   Da Ai (pronounced *dah eye*)
   Da Ai Da Ai Da Ai
   Da Ai Da Ai Da Ai
   Da Ai Da Ai Da Ai
   Da Ai Da Ai Da Ai Da Ai

   As you chant these five lines, inhale quickly after each line and visualize the golden light ball rotating as follows:

   When you chant line 1, the golden light ball rotates up from the first Soul House to the heart, then over to the heart chakra (fourth Soul House), and down through the Kun Gong back to the first Soul House.

   When you chant lines 2 through 5, the golden light ball rotates up from the first Soul House to the heart, then over to the heart chakra (fourth Soul House), and down through the Kun Gong back to the first Soul House. Then, the golden ball makes a circle. It goes from the first Soul House into the spinal cord through an invisible hole in front of the tailbone, then flows up the spinal cord to the occipital area, and then goes into and through the brain up to the crown chakra (seventh Soul House) atop your head. From there, it goes back down inside your nasal cavity to the palate, and then down through the fifth, fourth, third, and second chakras (Soul Houses) back to the root chakra (first Soul House). See figure 14 on page 88.

c. Repeat steps 3a and 3b for a total of four times.

You may chant aloud or silently. Doing both yang and yin chanting every time you practice is best.

Tao Calligraphy Power. Trace *Da Ai*, greatest love. You may trace *Da Ai* on the back cover. (See also "How to find other Tao Calligraphies in order to apply Tao Calligraphy Power" on page 59 above.)

When you trace, tracing becomes your Body Power. You may combine tracing with Mind Power, Sound Power, and/or Breath Power if you wish, or you may simply focus on tracing.

Close. End your practice session by saying:

Hao. Hao. Hao.
Thank you. Thank you. Thank you.

ဆ ဆ ဆ

We have applied six sacred Tao power techniques to heal and transform the spiritual body through Da Ai, greatest love. Da Ai is the first of the Ten Da. You can apply any of the other nine of the Da qualities in the same way for transforming the spiritual body.

Practice. Practice. Practice.

Experience the transformation.

8

Seven Energy Chakras (Soul Houses) and Wai Jiao

THE TEACHING OF CHAKRAS is recorded in the early traditions of Hinduism. They are spiritual energy centers that are the focus of many ancient meditations and practices. There are seven primary chakras.

I received the divine teaching in 2008 that the seven chakras are also the seven houses of the soul in a human being. They are in the core and central channel of the body. See figure 14 on page 88.

Each Soul House is fist sized. From lowest to highest, they are:

- first—at the pelvic floor, just above the perineum, which is the area between the anus and the scrotum or vulva, and the Hui Yin acupuncture point[16] (root chakra)
- second—in the lower abdomen, between the first and third Soul Houses (sacral chakra)
- third—at the level of the navel (navel chakra)
- fourth—the Message Center (heart chakra) in the middle of the chest
- fifth—in the throat (throat chakra)
- sixth—in the brain (third eye chakra)

---

[16] The Hui Yin acupuncture point lies on the perineum, midway between the anus and the scrotum or vulva. See figure 14 on page 88.

- seventh—atop the head on the Bai Hui acupuncture point[17] (crown chakra)

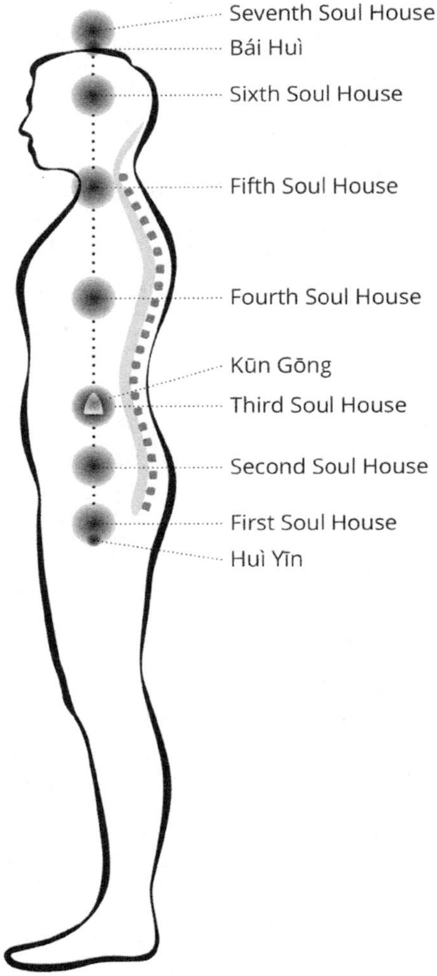

Figure 14. Seven chakras (Soul Houses) of a human being

[17] The Bai Hui acupuncture point is on the crown of the head, midway between the ears and midway between the front and back. See figure 14.

Power and significance of the seven chakras (Soul Houses) and Wai Jiao

The first Soul House is the origin, base, and root. It is the generating source of energy and light. On the physical level, this area is also the generator of life and energy. It is the engine that produces the driving force to generate and propel energy through the remaining six Soul Houses and through the entire body.

The first Soul House is exactly that; it is the first house in which a soul resides on its journey. It is the beginning of the soul journey. A human being's soul has been on its journey for many, many lifetimes. If your soul sits in the first Soul House, your soul is still at the beginning stages of the journey. The first Soul House is very important, but in your soul journey your soul needs to move to the higher Soul Houses.

The second Soul House is in the lower abdomen at the same level as the Lower Dan Tian,[18] between the first Soul House and the level of the navel. See figure 15. The second Soul House is important in the soul journey because when your soul reaches this position it has gained great virtue, which is Heaven's reward for positive information or messages that you have created. This virtue nourishes and uplifts your soul and is recorded in your book in the Akashic Records.[19] Your soul has made significant progress, but it still has a very long journey ahead.

The second Soul House is connected with the well-being and balance of the foundational energy of the Lower Dan Tian. It is connected with the well-being and balance of all creation. As in the big universe (nature), so too in the small universe (human being). As I revealed in *The Power of*

---

[18] The Lower Dan Tian is a fist sized foundational energy center in the lower abdomen. (See figure 15 on page 90.) It is a storehouse for energy. A powerful Lower Dan Tian is key for energy, stamina, vitality, immunity, rejuvenation, and longevity.

[19] The Akashic Records is the place in Heaven where all of one's actions, behaviors, speech, and thoughts, positive and negative, from all lifetimes are recorded. Every soul has a book in the Akashic Records.

Soul,[20] the authoritative book of my entire Soul Power Series, the lower abdomen is also a secret soul center of soul intelligence, wisdom, and knowledge.

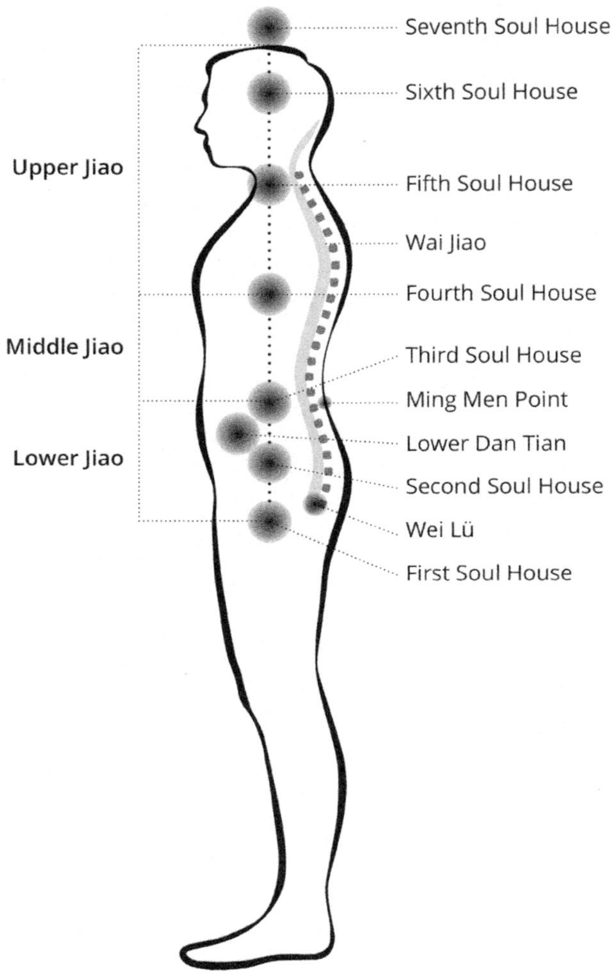

Figure 15. Seven Soul Houses, San Jiao, Wai Jiao, Ming Men point, Lower Dan Tian, and Wei Lü

[20] Dr. and Master Zhi Gang Sha, *The Power of Soul: The Way to Heal, Rejuvenate, and Enlighten All Life,* New York/Toronto: Atria Books/Heaven's Library Publication Corp., 2009.

In this area, message, energy, and matter circulate actively, influencing every aspect of one's being. The second Soul House connects with all of these aspects of all creation, including the Soul World, Divine, and Tao Source.

The third Soul House is important because it is the last one for a soul to pass through on its journey to enlightenment. When your soul reaches this level, it has made real progress. Souls are quite happy to have moved to this level. They are very eager to advance further because they know the next step is their enlightenment.

The fourth Soul House is very special. When your soul sits in the Message Center or heart chakra behind the lower end of the sternum, it has reached the level of enlightenment. Its soul standing has changed significantly. Reaching soul enlightenment usually requires hundreds or thousands of lifetimes.

Being enlightened transforms the quality of service you can offer. Your ability to serve becomes higher and more powerful. At the same time, your book in the Akashic Records is transferred to a special hall for those who are enlightened. Your ability to communicate with the Soul World increases significantly. The teachings, wisdom, and practices you receive from the Divine and the entire Soul World will be on an entirely different level. It is a major milestone on the soul journey, but it is only the beginning of the enlightenment journey.

The fourth Soul House is the center for healing, love, forgiveness, compassion, soul communication, transformation, enlightenment, and much more. All of these qualities also affect your physical journey. When your soul sits in the fourth Soul House, many blockages could be removed. Your well-being, including your physical, emotional, and mental health, could improve in a powerful way.

The fifth Soul House is in the throat. The souls of very few people reach this level through their own efforts. This Soul House is a bridge between the heart and the mind. It helps to integrate the wisdom of the heart and the mind. When this happens, the service you can give increases significantly again. Your ability to understand your own soul journey and that of others increases greatly.

On the physical level, the blessings bring about not only greater healing in every aspect of life but also substantial rejuvenation and prolongation of life. For many people, this Soul House is connected with soul memories. Healing of these memories can take place on a very deep level. As this happens, reversal of physical issues often occurs at an accelerated rate.

The sixth Soul House is in the brain. As the soul reaches this level, consciousness is transformed. The connection and alignment with divine consciousness are much stronger. The ability to communicate with the Soul World grows further. On the physical level, when a soul resides in the brain, it heals and rejuvenates every aspect of the physical body in a special way. The brain determines, directs, or influences every function of the body. When the soul resides in the brain, the brain's influence has reached a level of divine presence and light.

The seventh Soul House is just above the head in the crown chakra. This is the highest position in soul standing. On the physical level, when your soul resides in the seventh Soul House, it has reached a position where it truly can be in charge. It is able to direct every aspect of your life in a powerful way, including the physical, mental, emotional, relationship, and financial aspects. It is a great honor and privilege that your soul can reach this Soul House. Very few have accomplished it through their own efforts.

The Wai Jiao 外焦 is the space in the body in front of the spinal column plus the cranial cavity. See figure 15. It is the largest space in the body. Because all energies, meridians, and channels of the body must go through the Wai Jiao, negative shen qi jing in the Wai Jiao can affect any organ, any part of the body, and any other space. Therefore, the Wai Jiao is a key for all healing and transformation.

Power and significance of healing and transforming the seven chakras (Soul Houses) and Wai Jiao

All seven Soul Houses connect with aspects of creation, with the balancing of yin and yang, and with the practice of the Divine and Tao Source. As you practice with the seven chakras (Soul Houses), you are connecting with the soul journeys of the Divine and of all universes. You are connecting with all humanity and Mother Earth. As your soul moves to higher and higher Soul Houses, this connection of you, humanity, Mother Earth, and the Divine becomes more and more concrete, practical, and real in your daily life. Words cannot fully express the benefits you receive. Your practice benefits humanity, Mother Earth, and all universes.

As you do the practices in chapters nine and ten, the chanting, singing, and tracing promote the most important spaces and the most important energy, matter, and soul circles and channels in the body. All of the energies, matters, and souls of all of your systems, organs, cells, and meridians will gather together to join these most important circles and channels. If this energy circle flows, all energy circles will follow. If this matter circle flows, all matter circles will follow. If this soul channel flows, all soul channels will follow. These are the Shen Qi Jing Channels that I will explain further in chapter ten.

Let us move on to apply the six sacred Tao power techniques to heal and transform the seven chakras (Soul Houses) and Wai Jiao. Study the videos that have been created for you with my chanting for all the major practices in this book. You may even practice along with the videos.

Practice well.

Experience the healing and transformation.

9

Apply Six Sacred Tao Power Techniques to Heal the Seven Energy Chakras (Soul Houses) and Wai Jiao

THE SEVEN CHAKRAS OR Soul Houses are the major spaces inside the body. A human body can be divided into two parts. One is the organs. The other is the spaces.

Think about the air in Mother Earth. In some countries or some parts of the world the air is very clean. In some parts of the world the air is polluted. Polluted air causes lung sickness and many other sicknesses. Clean air is priceless.

In the body, cleaning the seven chakras or Soul Houses and Wai Jiao is just like cleaning the air in the spaces. Cleaning the space is a sacred way to heal the systems, organs, and cells. This is invaluable wisdom for every human being.

Let us apply the six sacred Tao power techniques to heal and transform the seven chakras (Soul Houses) and Wai Jiao. We will use a special Body Power hand position, the Yin Yang Palm, in the practices for the first three Soul Houses.

Yin Yang Palm

Grasp your left thumb with the fingers of your right hand and make a fist with your right hand. Wrap all four fingers of the left hand over the right hand. Grip your left thumb with about seventy-five to eighty percent of your maximum strength. This is the Yin Yang Palm hand position. See figure 16.

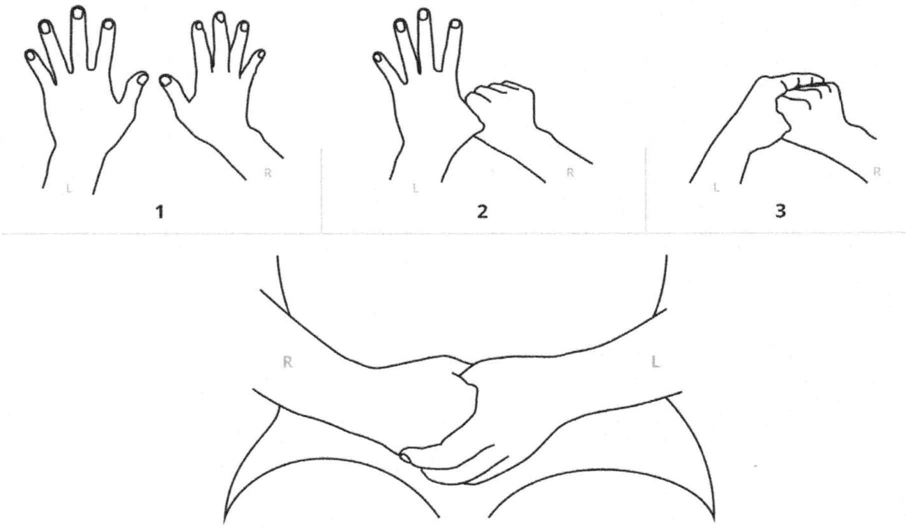

Figure 16. Yin Yang Palm hand position

First chakra or Soul House

Body Power. Place your hands in the Yin Yang Palm position over the first Soul House at the bottom of your torso.

Soul Power. Say *hello* to inner souls:

Dear soul heart mind body of my first chakra and Soul House,
I love you, honor you, and appreciate you.
You have the power to heal and rejuvenate yourselves.
Do a good job.
Thank you.

Say *hello* to outer souls:

Dear Tao Source and Divine,
Dear buddhas, saints (name the saints you believe in),
Dear Heaven, Mother Earth, and countless planets, stars, galaxies, and universes,
I love you, honor you, and appreciate you.
Please forgive my ancestors and me for all the mistakes we have made in all lifetimes related to the first Soul House.
I am sincerely sorry for all these mistakes.
I apologize from the bottom of my heart to all the souls my ancestors and I have hurt or harmed in these ways.
In order to be forgiven, I will serve unconditionally.
To chant and meditate is to serve.
I will chant and meditate as much as I can.
I will offer unconditional service as much as I can.
I unconditionally forgive anyone who hurt or harmed my ancestors or me in all lifetimes.
I am extremely grateful.
Thank you.

Mind Power. Visualize golden light shining in and around the first Soul House.

Breath Power. Inhale and expand your abdomen. Exhale and contract your abdomen. Make sure you inhale and exhale smoothly, evenly, and naturally. Remember that the length of each inhalation and exhalation depends on your personal condition. Follow nature's way.

Sound Power. As we chant, we combine the Sound Power with Breath Power and a more refined Mind Power visualization. See the video with my chanting that has been created for you for this practice and all the major practices in this book.

Step 1

a. Inhale. Visualize golden light going from your nose down through the center of your body and gathering as a ball in your first Soul House.

b. Exhale. Chant "Hei" (pronounced *hay*), the sacred sound for the first Soul House. At the same time, visualize the golden light ball rotating and exploding in all directions from the first Soul House.

c. Repeat steps 1a and 1b for a total of seven times.

Step 2

a. Inhale. Visualize golden light going from your nose down through the center of your body and gathering as a ball in your first Soul House.

b. Exhale. Chant "Hei Hei Hei." Visualize the golden light ball rotating and exploding in all directions from the first Soul House.

c. Repeat steps 2a and 2b for a total of four times.

Step 3

a. Inhale. Same visualization as in steps 1a and 2a.

b. Exhale. Chant:

   Hei Ya (pronounced *hay yah*)
   Hei Ya Hei Ya You (pronounced *hay yah hay yah yō*)
   Hei Ya Hei Ya You
   Hei Ya Hei Ya Hei Ya You
   Hei Ya Hei Ya Hei Ya Hei Ya You

   As you chant these five lines, inhale quickly after each line and visualize the golden light ball rotating as follows:

   When you chant line 1, the golden light ball rotates up from the first Soul House to the Kun Gong (inside the body behind the navel), then back down to the first Soul House.

   When you chant lines 2 through 5, the golden light ball rotates up from the first Soul House to the Kun Gong (inside the body behind the navel), then back down to the first Soul House. When you chant "You" in these lines, visualize the golden ball making a circle. It goes into the spinal cord through an invisible hole in front of the tailbone, then flows up the spinal cord to the occipital area, and then goes into and through the brain up to the seventh Soul House. From there, it goes back down inside your nasal cavity to the palate, and then down through the fifth, fourth, third, and second Soul Houses back to the first Soul House.

c. Repeat steps 3a and 3b for a total of four times.

You may chant aloud or silently. Doing both yang and yin chanting every time you practice is best.

Tao Calligraphy Power. Trace *Da Ai,* greatest love, or *Da Kuan Shu,* greatest forgiveness. (See "How to find other Tao Calligraphies in order to apply Tao Calligraphy Power" on page 59 above.)

When you trace, tracing becomes your Body Power. You may combine tracing with Mind Power, Sound Power, and/or Breath Power if you wish, or you may simply focus on tracing.

Close. End your practice session by saying:

Hao. Hao. Hao.
Thank you. Thank you. Thank you.

Second chakra or Soul House

Body Power. Place your hands in the Yin Yang Palm position over the second Soul House, on the lower abdomen below the navel.

Soul Power. Say *hello* to inner souls:

Dear soul heart mind body of my second chakra and Soul House,
I love you, honor you, and appreciate you.
You have the power to heal and rejuvenate yourselves.
Do a good job.
Thank you.

Say *hello* to outer souls:

Dear Tao Source and Divine,
Dear buddhas, saints (name the saints you believe in),

Dear Heaven, Mother Earth, and countless planets, stars, galaxies, and universes,
I love you, honor you, and appreciate you.
Please forgive my ancestors and me for all the mistakes we have made in all lifetimes related to the second Soul House.
I am sincerely sorry for all these mistakes.
I apologize from the bottom of my heart to all the souls my ancestors and I have hurt or harmed in these ways.
In order to be forgiven, I will serve unconditionally.
To chant and meditate is to serve.
I will chant and meditate as much as I can.
I will offer unconditional service as much as I can.
I unconditionally forgive anyone who hurt or harmed my ancestors or me in all lifetimes.
I am extremely grateful.
Thank you.

Mind Power. Visualize golden light shining in and around the second Soul House.

Breath Power. Inhale and expand your abdomen. Exhale and contract your abdomen. Make sure you inhale and exhale smoothly, evenly, and naturally. Remember that the length of each inhalation and exhalation depends on your personal condition. Follow nature's way.

Sound Power. As we chant, we combine the Sound Power with Breath Power and a more refined Mind Power visualization.

Step 1

a. Inhale. Visualize golden light going from your nose down through the center of your body and gathering as a ball in your first Soul House.

b. Exhale. Chant "Heng" (pronounced *hung*), the sacred sound for the second Soul House. At the same time, the golden light ball rotates up from the first Soul House to the second Soul House, where it rotates and explodes in all directions.

c. Repeat steps 1a and 1b for a total of seven times.

Step 2

a. Inhale. Visualize golden light going from your nose down through the center of your body and gathering as a ball in your first Soul House.

b. Exhale. Chant "Heng Heng Heng." The golden light ball rotates up from the first Soul House to the second Soul House, where it rotates and explodes in all directions.

c. Repeat steps 2a and 2b for a total of four times.

Step 3

a. Inhale. The golden light ball forms in your first Soul House.

b. Exhale. Chant:

   Heng Ya (pronounced *hung yah*)
   Heng Ya Heng Ya You (pronounced *hung yah hung yah yō*)
   Heng Ya Heng Ya You
   Heng Ya Heng Ya Heng Ya You
   Heng Ya Heng Ya Heng Ya Heng Ya You

   As you chant these five lines, inhale quickly after each line and visualize the golden light ball rotating as follows:

   When you chant line 1, the golden light ball rotates up from the first Soul House through the second Soul House to the Kun Gong, then returns down to the first Soul House.

   When you chant lines 2 through 5, the golden light ball rotates up from the first Soul House through the second Soul House to the Kun Gong, then returns to the first Soul House. When you chant "You" in these lines, visualize the golden ball making a circle. It goes into the spinal cord through an invisible hole in front of the tailbone, then flows up the spinal cord to the occipital area, and then goes into and through the brain up to the seventh Soul House. From there, it goes back down inside your nasal cavity to the palate, and then down through the fifth, fourth, third, and second Soul Houses back to the first Soul House.

c. Repeat steps 3a and 3b for a total of four times.

You may chant aloud or silently. Doing both yang and yin chanting every time you practice is best.

Tao Calligraphy Power. Trace *Da Ai*, greatest love, or *Da Kuan Shu*, greatest forgiveness. (See "How to find other Tao Calligraphies in order to apply Tao Calligraphy Power" on page 59 above.)

When you trace, tracing becomes your Body Power. You may combine tracing with Mind Power, Sound Power, and/or Breath Power if you wish, or you may simply focus on tracing.

Close. End your practice session by saying:

Hao. Hao. Hao.
Thank you. Thank you. Thank you.

Third chakra or Soul House

Body Power. Place your hands in the Yin Yang Palm position over the navel, which is also over the third Soul House.

Soul Power. Say *hello* to inner souls:

Dear soul heart mind body of my third chakra and Soul House,
I love you, honor you, and appreciate you.
You have the power to heal and rejuvenate yourselves.
Do a good job.
Thank you.

Say *hello* to outer souls:

Dear Tao Source and Divine,
Dear buddhas, saints (name the saints you believe in),
Dear Heaven, Mother Earth, and countless planets, stars, galaxies, and universes,
I love you, honor you, and appreciate you.
Please forgive my ancestors and me for all the mistakes we have made in all lifetimes related to the third Soul House.
I am sincerely sorry for all these mistakes.

I apologize from the bottom of my heart to all the souls my ancestors and I have hurt or harmed in these ways.
In order to be forgiven, I will serve unconditionally.
To chant and meditate is to serve.
I will chant and meditate as much as I can.
I will offer unconditional service as much as I can.
I unconditionally forgive anyone who hurt or harmed my ancestors or me in all lifetimes.
I am extremely grateful.
Thank you.

Mind Power. Visualize golden light shining in and around the third Soul House.

Breath Power. Inhale and expand your abdomen. Exhale and contract your abdomen. Make sure you inhale and exhale smoothly, evenly, and naturally. Remember that the length of each inhalation and exhalation depends on your personal condition. Follow nature's way.

Sound Power. As we chant, we combine the Sound Power with Breath Power and a more refined Mind Power visualization.

Step 1

a. Inhale. Visualize golden light going from your nose down through the center of your body and gathering as a ball in your first Soul House.
b. Exhale. Chant "Hong" (pronounced *hōng*), the sacred sound for the third Soul House. At the same time, the golden light ball rotates up from the first Soul House to the third Soul House, where it rotates and explodes in all directions.
c. Repeat steps 1a and 1b for a total of seven times.

Step 2

a. Inhale. Visualize golden light going from your nose down through the center of your body and gathering as a ball in your first Soul House.

b. Exhale. Chant "Hong Hong Hong." The golden light ball rotates up from the first Soul House to the third Soul House, where it rotates and explodes in all directions.

c. Repeat steps 2a and 2b for a total of four times.

Step 3

a. Inhale. The golden light ball forms in your first Soul House.

b. Exhale. Chant:

   Hong Ya (pronounced *hōng yah*)
   Hong Ya Hong Ya You (pronounced *hōng yah hōng yah yō*)
   Hong Ya Hong Ya You
   Hong Ya Hong Ya Hong Ya You
   Hong Ya Hong Ya Hong Ya Hong Ya You

   As you chant these five lines, inhale quickly after each line and visualize the golden light ball rotating as follows:

   When you chant line 1, the golden light ball rotates up from the first Soul House through the second Soul House to the third Soul House, then returns down to the first Soul House.

   When you chant lines 2 through 5, the golden light ball rotates up from the first Soul House through the second Soul House to the third Soul House, then returns to the first Soul House. When you chant "You" in these lines, visualize the golden ball making a circle. It goes into the spinal cord through an invisible hole in front of the tailbone, then flows up the spinal cord to the occipital area, and then goes into and through the brain up to the seventh Soul House. From there, it goes back down inside your nasal cavity to the palate, and then down through the fifth, fourth, third, and second Soul Houses back to the first Soul House.

c. Repeat steps 3a and 3b for a total of four times.

You may chant aloud or silently. Doing both yang and yin chanting every time you practice is best.

Tao Calligraphy Power. Trace *Da Ai,* greatest love, or *Da Kuan Shu,* greatest forgiveness. (See "How to find other Tao Calligraphies in order to apply Tao Calligraphy Power" on page 59 above.)

When you trace, tracing becomes your Body Power. You may combine tracing with Mind Power, Sound Power, and/or Breath Power if you wish, or you may simply focus on tracing.

Close. End your practice session by saying:

Hao. Hao. Hao.
Thank you. Thank you. Thank you.

Fourth chakra or Soul House

Body Power. Place one palm below the navel. Place the other palm over your Message Center.

Soul Power. Say *hello* to inner souls:

Dear soul heart mind body of my fourth Soul House,
I love you, honor you, and appreciate you.
You have the power to heal and rejuvenate yourselves.
Do a good job.
Thank you.

Say *hello* to outer souls:

Dear Tao Source and Divine,
Dear buddhas, saints (name the saints you believe in),
Dear Heaven, Mother Earth, and countless planets, stars, galaxies, and universes,
I love you, honor you, and appreciate you.
Please forgive my ancestors and me for all the mistakes we have made in all lifetimes related to the fourth Soul House.
I am sincerely sorry for all these mistakes.
I apologize from the bottom of my heart to all the souls my ancestors and I have hurt or harmed in these ways.
In order to be forgiven, I will serve unconditionally.

To chant and meditate is to serve.
I will chant and meditate as much as I can.
I will offer unconditional service as much as I can.
I unconditionally forgive anyone who hurt or harmed my ancestors or me in all lifetimes.
I am extremely grateful.
Thank you.

Mind Power. Visualize golden light shining in and around the fourth Soul House.

Breath Power. Inhale and expand your abdomen. Exhale and contract your abdomen. Make sure you inhale and exhale smoothly, evenly, and naturally. Remember that the length of each inhalation and exhalation depends on your personal condition. Follow nature's way.

Sound Power. As we chant, we combine the Sound Power with Breath Power and a more refined Mind Power visualization.

Step 1

a. Inhale. Visualize golden light going from your nose down through the center of your body and gathering as a ball in your first Soul House.

b. Exhale. Chant "Ah," the sacred sound for the fourth Soul House. At the same time, the golden light ball rotates up from the first Soul House to the fourth Soul House, where it rotates and explodes in all directions.

c. Repeat steps 1a and 1b for a total of seven times.

Step 2

a. Inhale. Visualize golden light going from your nose down through the center of your body and gathering as a ball in your first Soul House.

b. Exhale. Chant "Ah Ah Ah." The golden light ball rotates up from the first Soul House through the second and third Soul Houses to the fourth Soul House, where it rotates and explodes in all directions.

c. Repeat steps 2a and 2b for a total of four times.

Step 3

a. Inhale. The golden light ball forms in your first Soul House.

b. Exhale. Chant:

Ah Ya (pronounced *ah yah*)
Ah Ya Ah Ya You (pronounced *ah yah ah yah yō*)
Ah Ya Ah Ya You
Ah Ya Ah Ya Ah Ya You
Ah Ya Ah Ya Ah Ya Ah Ya You

As you chant these five lines, inhale quickly after each line and visualize the golden light ball rotating as follows:

When you chant line 1, the golden light ball rotates up from the first Soul House to the fourth Soul House, then returns down through the Kun Gong to the first Soul House.

When you chant lines 2 through 5, the golden light ball rotates up from the first Soul House to the fourth Soul House, then returns down through the Kun Gong to the first Soul House. When you chant "You" in these lines, visualize the golden ball making a circle. It goes into the spinal cord through an invisible hole in front of the tailbone, then flows up the spinal cord to the occipital area, and then goes into and through the brain up to the seventh Soul House. From there, it goes back down inside your nasal cavity to the palate, and then down through the fifth, fourth, third, and second Soul Houses back to the first Soul House.

c. Repeat steps 3a and 3b for a total of four times.

You may chant aloud or silently. Doing both yang and yin chanting every time you practice is best.

Tao Calligraphy Power. Trace *Da Ai,* greatest love, or *Da Kuan Shu,* greatest forgiveness. (See "How to find other Tao Calligraphies in order to apply Tao Calligraphy Power" on page 59 above.)

When you trace, tracing becomes your Body Power. You may combine tracing with Mind Power, Sound Power, and/or Breath Power if you wish, or you may simply focus on tracing.

Close. End your practice session by saying:

Hao. Hao. Hao.
Thank you. Thank you. Thank you.

Fifth chakra or Soul House

Body Power. Place one palm below the navel. Place the other palm on your throat, over the fifth Soul House.

Soul Power. Say *hello* to inner souls:

Dear soul heart mind body of my fifth Soul House,
I love you, honor you, and appreciate you.
You have the power to heal and rejuvenate yourselves.
Do a good job.
Thank you.

Say *hello* to outer souls:

Dear Tao Source and Divine,
Dear buddhas, saints (name the saints you believe in),
Dear Heaven, Mother Earth, and countless planets, stars, galaxies, and universes,
I love you, honor you, and appreciate you.
Please forgive my ancestors and me for all the mistakes we have made in all lifetimes related to the fifth Soul House.
I am sincerely sorry for all these mistakes.
I apologize from the bottom of my heart to all the souls my ancestors and I have hurt or harmed in these ways.
In order to be forgiven, I will serve unconditionally.
To chant and meditate is to serve.
I will chant and meditate as much as I can.
I will offer unconditional service as much as I can.

I unconditionally forgive anyone who hurt or harmed my ancestors or me in all lifetimes.
I am extremely grateful.
Thank you.

Mind Power. Visualize golden light shining in and around the fifth Soul House.

Breath Power. Inhale and expand your abdomen. Exhale and contract your abdomen. Make sure you inhale and exhale smoothly, evenly, and naturally. Remember that the length of each inhalation and exhalation depends on your personal condition. Follow nature's way.

Sound Power. As we chant, we combine the Sound Power with Breath Power and a more refined Mind Power visualization.

Step 1

a. Inhale. Visualize golden light going from your nose down through the center of your body and gathering as a ball in your first Soul House.

b. Exhale. Chant "Xi" (pronounced *shee*), the sacred sound for the fifth Soul House. At the same time, the golden light ball rotates up from the first Soul House to the fifth Soul House, where it rotates and explodes in all directions.

c. Repeat steps 1a and 1b for a total of seven times.

Step 2

d. Inhale. Visualize golden light going from your nose down through the center of your body and gathering as a ball in your first Soul House.

e. Exhale. Chant "Xi Xi Xi." The golden light ball rotates up from the first Soul House through the second, third, and fourth Soul Houses to the fifth Soul House, where it rotates and explodes in all directions.

f. Repeat steps 2a and 2b for a total of four times.

Step 3

a. Inhale. The golden light ball forms in your first Soul House.

b. Exhale. Chant:

Xi Ya (pronounced *shee yah*)
Xi Ya Xi Ya You (pronounced *shee yah shee yah yō*)
Xi Ya Xi Ya You
Xi Ya Xi Ya Xi Ya You
Xi Ya Xi Ya Xi Ya Xi Ya You

As you chant these five lines, inhale quickly after each line and visualize the golden light ball rotating as follows:

When you chant line 1, the golden light ball rotates up from the first Soul House to the fifth Soul House, then returns down through the Kun Gong to the first Soul House.

When you chant lines 2 through 5, the golden light ball rotates up from the first Soul House to the fifth Soul House, then returns down through the Kun Gong to the first Soul House. When you chant "You" in these lines, visualize the golden ball making a circle. It goes into the spinal cord through an invisible hole in front of the tailbone, then flows up the spinal cord to the occipital area, and then goes into and through the brain up to the seventh Soul House. From there, it goes back down inside your nasal cavity to the palate, and then down through the fifth, fourth, third, and second Soul Houses back to the first Soul House.

c. Repeat steps 3a and 3b for a total of four times.

You may chant aloud or silently. Doing both yang and yin chanting every time you practice is best.

Tao Calligraphy Power. Trace *Da Ai,* greatest love, or *Da Kuan Shu,* greatest forgiveness. (See "How to find other Tao Calligraphies in order to apply Tao Calligraphy Power" on page 59 above.)

When you trace, tracing becomes your Body Power. You may combine tracing with Mind Power, Sound Power, and/or Breath Power if you wish, or you may simply focus on tracing.

Close. End your practice session by saying:

Hao. Hao. Hao.
Thank you. Thank you. Thank you.

Sixth chakra or Soul House

Body Power. Place one palm below the navel. Place the other palm on your forehead, over the sixth Soul House.

Soul Power. Say *hello* to inner souls:

Dear soul heart mind body of my sixth Soul House,
I love you, honor you, and appreciate you.
You have the power to heal and rejuvenate yourselves.
Do a good job.
Thank you.

Say *hello* to outer souls:

Dear Tao Source and Divine,
Dear buddhas, saints (name the saints you believe in),
Dear Heaven, Mother Earth, and countless planets, stars, galaxies, and universes,
I love you, honor you, and appreciate you.
Please forgive my ancestors and me for all the mistakes we have made in all lifetimes related to the sixth Soul House.
I am sincerely sorry for all these mistakes.
I apologize from the bottom of my heart to all the souls my ancestors and I have hurt or harmed in these ways.
In order to be forgiven, I will serve unconditionally.
To chant and meditate is to serve.
I will chant and meditate as much as I can.
I will offer unconditional service as much as I can.
I unconditionally forgive anyone who hurt or harmed my ancestors or me in all lifetimes.
I am extremely grateful.
Thank you.

Mind Power. Visualize golden light shining in and around the sixth Soul House.

Breath Power. Inhale and expand your abdomen. Exhale and contract your abdomen. Make sure you inhale and exhale smoothly, evenly, and naturally. Remember that the length of each inhalation and exhalation depends on your personal condition. Follow nature's way.

Sound Power. As we chant, we combine the Sound Power with Breath Power and a more refined Mind Power visualization.

Step 1

a. Inhale. Visualize golden light going from your nose down through the center of your body and gathering as a ball in your first Soul House.
b. Exhale. Chant "Yi" (pronounced *yee*), the sacred sound for the sixth Soul House. At the same time, the golden light ball rotates up from the first Soul House to the sixth Soul House, where it rotates and explodes in all directions.
c. Repeat steps 1a and 1b for a total of seven times.

Step 2

a. Inhale. Visualize golden light going from your nose down through the center of your body and gathering as a ball in your first Soul House.
b. Exhale. Chant "Yi Yi Yi." The golden light ball rotates up from the first Soul House through the second, third, fourth, and fifth Soul Houses to the sixth Soul House, where it rotates and explodes in all directions.
c. Repeat steps 2a and 2b for a total of four times.

Step 3

a. Inhale. The golden light ball forms in your first Soul House.
b. Exhale. Chant:

   Yi Ya (pronounced *yee yah*)

Yi Ya Yi Ya You (pronounced *yee yah yee yah yō*)
Yi Ya Yi Ya You
Yi Ya Yi Ya Yi Ya You
Yi Ya Yi Ya Yi Ya Yi Ya You

As you chant these five lines, inhale quickly after each line and visualize the golden light ball rotating as follows:

When you chant line 1, the golden light ball rotates up from the first Soul House to the sixth Soul House, then returns down through the Kun Gong to the first Soul House.

When you chant lines 2 through 5, the golden light ball rotates up from the first Soul House to the sixth Soul House, then returns down through the Kun Gong to the first Soul House. When you chant "You" in these lines, visualize the golden ball making a circle. It goes into the spinal cord through an invisible hole in front of the tailbone, then flows up the spinal cord to the occipital area, and then goes into and through the brain up to the seventh Soul House. From there, it goes back down inside your nasal cavity to the palate, and then down through the fifth, fourth, third, and second Soul Houses back to the first Soul House.

c. Repeat steps 3a and 3b for a total of four times.

You may chant aloud or silently. Doing both yang and yin chanting every time you practice is best.

Tao Calligraphy Power. Trace *Da Ai,* greatest love, or *Da Kuan Shu,* greatest forgiveness. (See "How to find other Tao Calligraphies in order to apply Tao Calligraphy Power" on page 59 above.)

When you trace, tracing becomes your Body Power. You may combine tracing with Mind Power, Sound Power, and/or Breath Power if you wish, or you may simply focus on tracing.

Close. End your practice session by saying:

Hao. Hao. Hao.
Thank you. Thank you. Thank you.

Seventh chakra or Soul House

Body Power. Place one palm below the navel. Place the other palm over the Bai Hui acupuncture point at the top of the head.

Soul Power. Say *hello* to inner souls:

Dear soul heart mind body of my seventh Soul House,
I love you, honor you, and appreciate you.
You have the power to heal and rejuvenate yourselves.
Do a good job.
Thank you.

Say *hello* to outer souls:

Dear Tao Source and Divine,
Dear buddhas, saints (name the saints you believe in),
Dear Heaven, Mother Earth, and countless planets, stars, galaxies, and universes,
I love you, honor you, and appreciate you.
Please forgive my ancestors and me for all the mistakes we have made in all lifetimes related to the seventh Soul House.
I am sincerely sorry for all these mistakes.
I apologize from the bottom of my heart to all the souls my ancestors and I have hurt or harmed in these ways.
In order to be forgiven, I will serve unconditionally.
To chant and meditate is to serve.
I will chant and meditate as much as I can.
I will offer unconditional service as much as I can.
I unconditionally forgive anyone who hurt or harmed my ancestors or me in all lifetimes.
I am extremely grateful.
Thank you.

Mind Power. Visualize golden light shining in and around the seventh Soul House.

Breath Power. Inhale and expand your abdomen. Exhale and contract your abdomen. Make sure you inhale and exhale smoothly, evenly, and naturally. Remember that the length of each inhalation and exhalation depends on your personal condition. Follow nature's way.

Sound Power. As we chant, we combine the Sound Power with Breath Power and a more refined Mind Power visualization.

Step 1

a. Inhale. Visualize golden light going from your nose down through the center of your body and gathering as a ball in your first Soul House.

b. Exhale. Chant "Weng" (pronounced *wung*), the sacred sound for the seventh Soul House. At the same time, the golden light ball rotates up from the first Soul House to the seventh Soul House, where it rotates explodes in all directions.

c. Repeat steps 1a and 1b for a total of seven times.

Step 2

a. Inhale. Visualize golden light going from your nose down through the center of your body and gathering as a ball in your first Soul House.

b. Exhale. Chant "Weng Weng Weng." The golden light ball rotates up from the first Soul House through the second, third, fourth, fifth, and sixth Soul Houses to the seventh Soul House, where it rotates and explodes in all directions.

c. Repeat steps 2a and 2b for a total of four times.

Step 3

a. Inhale. The golden light ball forms in your first Soul House.

b. Exhale. Chant:

   Weng Ya (pronounced *wung yah*)
   Weng Ya Weng Ya You (pronounced *wung yah wung yah yō*)
   Weng Ya Weng Ya You
   Weng Ya Weng Ya Weng Ya You
   Weng Ya Weng Ya Weng Ya Weng Ya You

As you chant these five lines, inhale quickly after each line and visualize the golden light ball rotating as follows:

When you chant line 1, the golden light ball rotates up from the first Soul House to the seventh Soul House, then returns down through the Kun Gong to the first Soul House.

When you chant lines 2 through 5, the golden light ball rotates up from the first Soul House to the seventh Soul House, then returns down through the Kun Gong to the first Soul House. When you chant "You" in these lines, visualize the golden ball making a circle. It goes into the spinal cord through an invisible hole in front of the tailbone, then flows up the spinal cord to the occipital area, and then goes into and through the brain up to the seventh Soul House. From there, it goes back down inside your nasal cavity to the palate, and then down through the fifth, fourth, third, and second Soul Houses back to the first Soul House.

c. Repeat steps 3a and 3b for a total of four times.

You may chant aloud or silently. Doing both yang and yin chanting every time you practice is best.

Tao Calligraphy Power. Trace *Da Ai*, greatest love, or *Da Kuan Shu*, greatest forgiveness. (See "How to find other Tao Calligraphies in order to apply Tao Calligraphy Power" on page 59 above.)

When you trace, tracing becomes your Body Power. You may combine tracing with Mind Power, Sound Power, and/or Breath Power if you wish, or you may simply focus on tracing.

Close. End your practice session by saying:

Hao. Hao. Hao.
Thank you. Thank you. Thank you.

Wai Jiao

Body Power. Place one palm below the navel. Place the other palm over the Ming Men acupuncture point, on the back directly behind the navel.

Soul Power. Say *hello* to inner souls:

Dear soul heart mind body of my Wai Jiao (pronounced *wye jee-yow*),
I love you, honor you, and appreciate you.
You have the power to heal and rejuvenate yourselves.
Do a good job.
Thank you.

Say *hello* to outer souls:

Dear Tao Source and Divine,
Dear buddhas, saints (name the saints you believe in),
Dear Heaven, Mother Earth, and countless planets, stars, galaxies, and universes,
I love you, honor you, and appreciate you.
Please forgive my ancestors and me for all the mistakes we have made in all lifetimes related to the Wai Jiao.
I am sincerely sorry for all these mistakes.
I apologize from the bottom of my heart to all the souls my ancestors and I have hurt or harmed in these ways.
In order to be forgiven, I will serve unconditionally.
To chant and meditate is to serve.
I will chant and meditate as much as I can.
I will offer unconditional service as much as I can.
I unconditionally forgive anyone who hurt or harmed my ancestors or me in all lifetimes.
I am extremely grateful.
Thank you.

Mind Power. Visualize golden light shining in and around your Wai Jiao.

Breath Power. Inhale and expand your abdomen. Exhale and contract your abdomen. Make sure you inhale and exhale smoothly, evenly, and naturally. Remember that the length of each inhalation and exhalation depends on your personal condition. Follow nature's way.

Sound Power. As we chant, we combine the Sound Power with Breath Power and a more refined Mind Power visualization.

Step 1

a. Inhale. Visualize golden light going from your nose down through the center of your body and gathering as a ball in your first Soul House.

b. Exhale. Chant "You," the sacred sound for the Wai Jiao and the Ming Men point. At the same time, the golden light ball rotates up from the first Soul House to the Ming Men point, where it rotates and explodes.

c. Repeat steps 1a and 1b for a total of seven times.

Step 2

a. Inhale. Visualize golden light going from your nose down through the center of your body and gathering as a ball in your first Soul House.

b. Exhale. Chant "You You You." The golden light ball rotates up from the first Soul House to the Ming Men point, where it rotates and explodes.

c. Repeat steps 2a and 2b for a total of four times.

Step 3

a. Inhale. The golden light ball forms in your first Soul House.

b. Exhale. Chant:

   You Ya (pronounced *yō yah*)
   You Ya You Ya You (pronounced *yō yah yō yah yō*)
   You Ya You Ya You
   You Ya You Ya You Ya You
   You Ya You Ya You Ya You Ya You

   As you chant these five lines, inhale quickly after each line and visualize the golden light ball rotating as follows:

When you chant line 1, the golden light ball rotates up from the first Soul House to the Ming Men point, then goes to the Kun Gong, and back down to the first Soul House.

When you chant lines 2 through 5, the golden light ball rotates up from the first Soul House to the Ming Men point, then goes to the Kun Gong, and back down to the first Soul House. When you chant "You" at the end of each of these lines, visualize the golden ball making a circle. From the first Soul House, it goes into the spinal cord through an invisible hole in front of the tailbone, then flows up the spinal cord to the occipital area, and then goes into and through the brain up to the seventh Soul House. From there, it goes back down inside your nasal cavity to the palate, and then down through the fifth, fourth, third, and second Soul Houses back to the first Soul House.

c. Repeat steps 3a and 3b for a total of four times.

You may chant aloud or silently. Doing both yang and yin chanting every time you practice is best.

Tao Calligraphy Power. Trace Da Ai, greatest love, or Da Kuan Shu, greatest forgiveness. (See "How to find other Tao Calligraphies in order to apply Tao Calligraphy Power" on page 59 above.)

When you trace, tracing becomes your Body Power. You may combine tracing with Mind Power, Sound Power, and/or Breath Power if you wish, or you may simply focus on tracing.

Close. End your practice session by saying:

Hao. Hao. Hao.
Thank you. Thank you. Thank you.

ഌ ഌ ഌ

This chapter has shared the sacred practices to heal and transform the seven chakras (Soul Houses) and the Wai Jiao by applying six sacred Tao power techniques.

Practice. Practice. Practice.

Experience the transformation.

10

Shen Qi Jing Channels

AS THE LAW OF Shen Qi Jing tells us, everyone and everything is made of shen qi jing. In the human body, there is a major channel for each of these three components of a being. The Shen Channel is the major soul channel. The Qi Channel is the major energy channel. The Jing Channel is the major matter channel. Because one's shen qi jing are interconnected and interrelated, all three play vital roles in healing and transformation. Cleanse, purify, strengthen, empower, and enlighten the Shen Qi Jing Channels to heal and transform every aspect of life.

Qi Channel

The Qi Channel is the major energy channel in a human body. See figure 17.

The Qi Channel starts at the Hui Yin acupuncture point on the perineum, at the base of the first Soul House. It moves up the central channel of the body through the second, third, fourth, fifth, and sixth Soul Houses to the Bai Hui acupuncture point on the crown of the head and at the base of the seventh Soul House. From there, the Qi Channel turns down through the Wai Jiao and returns to the first Soul House. The Wai Jiao is the space in front of the spinal column plus the space in the head. It is the biggest space in the body. See figure 15 on page 90.

Note that the Qi Channel is unidirectional. Proper flow of qi in this channel is in the direction described above and indicated by the arrowheads in figure 17.

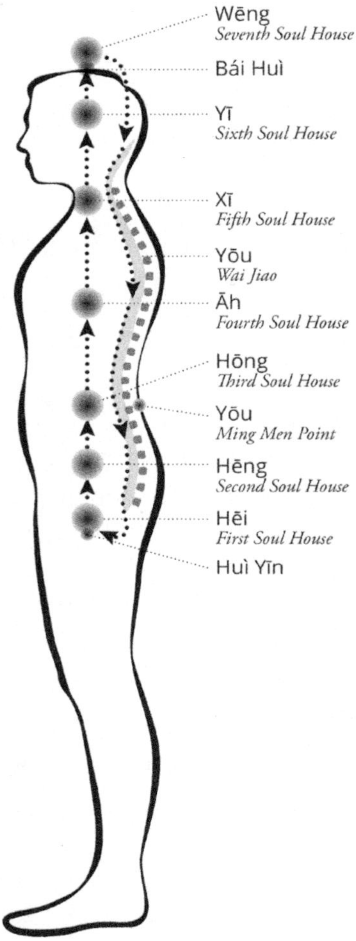

Figure 17. Qi Channel

The Qi Channel is the key for healing all sickness.

The sacred and secret mantra of the Qi Channel is:

Hei Heng Hong Ah Xi Yi Weng You
嘿哼哄啊唏噎嗡呦

The Qi Channel is the pathway of the seven Soul Houses, the San Jiao, and the Wai Jiao. Hei Heng Hong Ah Xi Yi Weng You assembles all the secret mantras on the pathway. Therefore, this mantra not only purifies and removes shen qi jing blockages from the Qi Channel, it also further removes shen qi jing blockages from and strengthens each Soul House, the San Jiao, and the Wai Jiao. The more you chant this mantra, the more benefits you will receive on this pathway.

Jing Channel

The Jing Channel is the major matter channel in a human body. It moves in the reverse direction of the Qi Channel. See figure 18 below.

Like the Qi Channel, the Jing Channel also starts at the Hui Yin acupuncture point on the perineum, but it then moves up and back to the tailbone, goes through an invisible hole in the tailbone, and connects with the spinal cord. It then goes up through the spinal cord to the brain and up to the Bai Hui acupuncture point on the crown of the head. From there it flows down the central channel through the sixth, fifth, fourth, third, second, and first Soul Houses, returning to the Hui Yin acupuncture point.

The Jing Channel is the key for rejuvenation and longevity.

The sacred and secret mantra of the Jing Channel is:

You Weng Yi Xi Ah Hong Heng Hei
呦嗡噎唏啊哄哼嘿

When you chant *You Weng Yi Xi Ah Hong Heng Hei*, you are cleansing the sacred pathway for rejuvenation and longevity. Because the Qi Channel and Jing Channel have similar pathways, the sacred Jing Channel mantra can also further remove shen qi jing blockages from and strengthen each Soul House, the San Jiao, and the Wai Jiao. Therefore, chant the Jing Channel mantra more to receive more benefits in these vital spaces of the body.

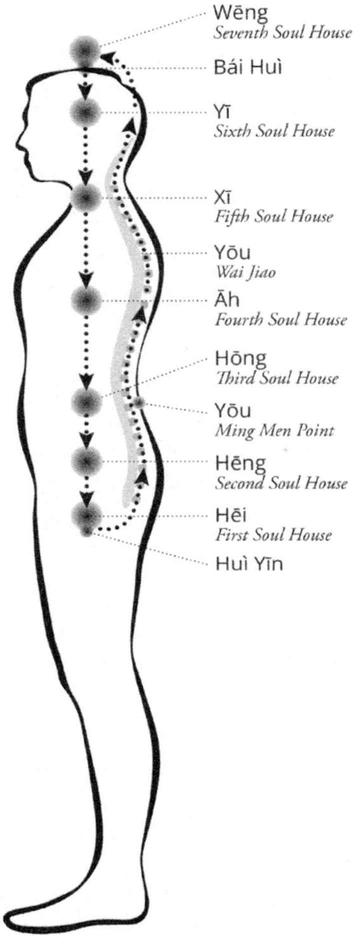

Figure 18. Jing Channel

Shen Channel

The Shen Channel is the immortality pathway. It starts simultaneously at two points: (1) the Bai Hui acupuncture point at the base of the seventh Soul House and (2) the Hui Yin acupuncture point at the base of the first Soul House. See figure 19 below.

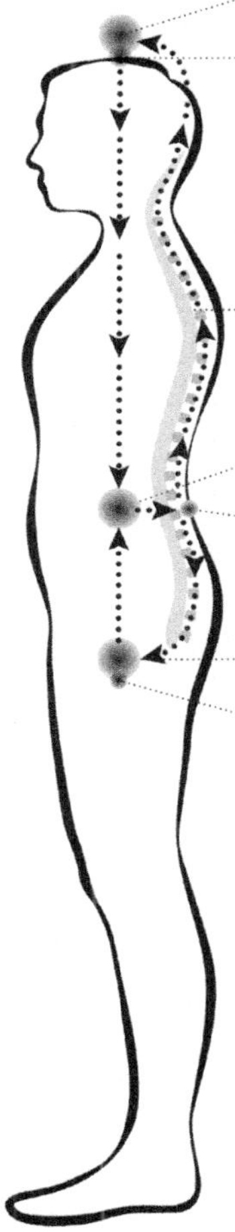

Figure 19. Shen Channel

The Bai Hui and Hui Yin acupuncture points are respectively the points where all the yang and all the yin in the body gather. As you have learned in the previous chapter, the secret mantras for these two points and the Soul Houses they support are Weng and Hei, respectively.

From the Bai Hui point at the top of the head and the Hui Yin point at the base of the torso, the Shen Channel flows through the central channel down from the seventh Soul House and, at the same time, up from the first Soul House to meet behind the navel in the third Soul House with the secret mantra Hong. From there, it flows as one straight back to the Ming Men acupuncture point[21] where it then splits. One part goes into the spinal cord and travels up, returning to the Bai Hui acupuncture point. The other part goes into the spinal cord and travels down, returning to the Hui Yin acupuncture point, all with the secret mantra You.

Therefore, the sacred and secret mantra of the Shen Channel is:

Weng Hei Hong You
嗡嘿哄呦

The secret mantra Weng connects with Heaven. The secret mantra Hei connects with Mother Earth. The secret mantra Hong connects with a human being. The secret mantra You connects with Tao. When you chant *Weng Hei Hong You*, the shen qi jing of Heaven, Mother Earth, human being, and Tao will join as one. When ren di tian Dao (*human being, Mother Earth, Heaven, Tao*) join as one, one reaches immortality. Therefore, this sacred mantra is to practice to achieve immortality.

Power and significance of Shen Qi Jing Channels

I will summarize the power and significance of these three channels.

- Qi Channel is for healing all sickness.
- Jing Channel is for rejuvenation and longevity.
- Shen Channel is for immortality.

When you practice with the Shen Qi Jing Channels there is no limitation. You can practice with each channel for a few minutes per time. You can practice with each channel for thirty minutes, one hour, or even longer. The longer you practice, the greater the benefits you could receive.

---

[21] "Ming" means *life*. "Men" means *gate*. The Ming Men acupuncture point is the "gate of life." It is located on the back, directly behind the navel. See figure 15 on page 90.

Practice. Practice. Practice.

Experience. Experience. Experience.

Let us now apply the six sacred Tao power techniques to heal and transform the Shen Qi Jing Channels.

Practice with Shen Qi Jing Channels to heal and transform

Body Power. Place your hands in the Yin Yang Palm position on your lower abdomen below the navel. See figure 16 on page 96.

Soul Power. Say *hello* to inner souls:

Dear soul heart mind body of my Shen Qi Jing Channels,
I love you, honor you, and appreciate you.
You have the power to purify and remove my shen qi jing blockages for healing, rejuvenation, prolonging life, and developing wisdom in every aspect of my life.
You have the power to fully open and develop yourselves.
Do a good job.
Thank you for blessing me
I am very grateful.

Say *hello* to outer souls:

Dear Tao Source and Divine,
Dear buddhas, saints (name the saints you believe in),
Dear Heaven, Mother Earth, and countless planets, stars, galaxies, and universes,
I love you, honor you, and appreciate you.
Please forgive my ancestors and me for all the mistakes we have made in all lifetimes related to the Shen Qi Jing Channels.
I am sincerely sorry for all these mistakes.
I apologize from the bottom of my heart to all the souls my ancestors and I have hurt or harmed in these ways.
In order to be forgiven, I will serve unconditionally.
To chant and meditate is to serve.

I will chant and meditate as much as I can.
I will offer unconditional service as much as I can.
I unconditionally forgive anyone who hurt or harmed my ancestors or me in all lifetimes.
I am extremely grateful.
Thank you.

Mind Power. Visualize golden light shining in and around the area for which you wish to receive healing and rejuvenation.

Breath Power. Inhale and expand your abdomen. Exhale and contract your abdomen. Make sure you inhale and exhale smoothly, evenly, and naturally. Remember that the length of each inhalation and exhalation depends on your personal condition.

Sound Power. As we chant, we combine the Sound Power with Breath Power and a more refined Mind Power visualization. See the video with my chanting that has been created for you for this practice and all the major practices in this book.

Qi Channel

a. Inhale. Visualize golden light going from your nose down through the center of your body and gathering as a ball in your first Soul House.

b. Exhale. Chant "Hei Heng Hong Ah Xi Yi Weng You" (pronounced *hey hung hōng ah shee yee wung yō*). At the same time, the golden ball follows the path of the Qi Channel, rotating up the central channel to the Bai Hui acupuncture point, and then down through the Wai Jiao, returning to the first Soul House.

c. Repeat the above steps four times.

Jing Channel

a. Inhale. Visualize golden light going from your nose down through the center of your body and gathering as a ball in your first Soul House.

b. Exhale. Chant "You Weng Yi Xi Ah Hong Heng Hei" (pronounced *yō wung yee shee ah hōng hung hay*). At the same time, the golden ball follows the path of the Jing Channel, rotating from the first Soul House back to the tailbone and into the spinal cord; then flows up the spinal cord and through the brain, reaching the Bai Hui acupuncture point. Then it flows down the central channel through the sixth, fifth, fourth, third, and second Soul Houses, returning to the first Soul House.

c. Repeat the above steps four times.

Shen Channel

a. Inhale. Golden light goes from your nose down through the center of your body and gathers as a ball in your first Soul House.

b. Exhale. Chant "Weng Hei Hong You" (pronounced *wung hay hōng yō*). The golden ball has subdivided into two golden balls: one at the Bai Hui acupuncture point at the base of the seventh Soul House and one at the Hui Yin acupuncture point at the base of the first Soul House. From these two points, the golden balls follow the path of the Shen Channel. They flow through the central channel down from the seventh Soul House and up from the first Soul House to join as one ball behind the navel in the third Soul House.

   From there, the golden ball flows straight back to the Ming Men acupuncture point where it splits into two balls, with one ball going up through the spinal cord, returning to the Bai Hui acupuncture point, and the other ball going down through the spinal cord, returning to the Hui Yin acupuncture point.

c. Repeat the above steps four times.

You may chant aloud or silently. Doing both yang and yin chanting every time you practice is best.

Tao Calligraphy Power. Trace *Da Ai,* greatest love, or *Da Kuan Shu,* greatest forgiveness. (See "How to find other Tao Calligraphies in order to apply Tao Calligraphy Power" on page 59 above.)

When you trace, tracing becomes your Body Power. You may combine tracing with Mind Power, Sound Power, and/or Breath Power if you wish, or you may simply focus on tracing.

Close. End your practice session by saying:

> *Hao. Hao. Hao.*
> *Thank you. Thank you. Thank you.*

ᜊ ᜊ ᜋ

You can practice for five to ten minutes per time. You can practice for thirty minutes, one hour, or longer. There is no time limit. The longer you practice, the more benefits you could receive.

Practice. Practice. Practice.

Experience the transformation.

11

Apply Six Sacred Tao Power Techniques to Heal and Transform Relationships

RELATIONSHIPS ARE A VERY important issue for humanity. Millions of people have good relationships. Millions of people have challenging relationships.

There are many different types of relationships, including relationships with a husband, a wife, children, parents, grandparents, grandchildren, bosses, colleagues, and friends. Each of us is deeply affected by relationships between various organizations and relationships between cities and countries. Some other extremely important personal relationships are your relationships with your physical spiritual teachers and with your spiritual fathers and mothers and other spiritual guides in Heaven.

Throughout a person's life there could be struggles with many blockages in relationships. Some people have difficulties with their parents. Others have difficulties with their children. Some people have difficulties with their colleagues or their bosses. People often wonder why they have these struggles.

It is a rare person who has not struggled at some time in life with a relationship. Some people struggle their whole lives with relationships. Some people can never find a true love, going through one divorce or breakup after another. Some children are abused by their parents. Some parents can be abused by their children. Other people can be cheated by their business partners. Relationship problems are very common on Mother Earth.

What is the root cause of blockages in relationships? In one sentence:

The root cause of blockages in relationships is negative shen qi jing from this lifetime and all past lifetimes.

You have the power to clear the negative shen qi jing blockages from past lifetimes and this lifetime in all of your relationships. Forgiveness is the key. To forgive and be forgiven for the relationship mistakes in past lives and in this life is to heal all of your relationships.

The sacred wisdom is that relationship blockages accumulate mainly within the Message Center (heart chakra or fourth Soul House). To balance the emotions in all kinds of relationships is to heal the negative shen qi jing of relationship blockages within the Message Center by transforming them into positive shen qi jing.

Now let us apply six sacred Tao power techniques to practice Da Kuan Shu, greatest forgiveness, to heal and transform relationships. I emphasize the power and significance of Da Kuan Shu:

Second of the Ten Da natures of Tao is greatest forgiveness.
I forgive you.
You forgive me.
Love, peace, and harmony.

Body Power. Place one palm over the Message Center. Place the other palm on the lower abdomen below the navel.

Soul Power. Say *hello* to your and the other person's inner souls:

> *Dear soul heart mind body of myself and of* (name the person[s] with whom you need relationship healing and transformation) *and dear soul heart mind body of my relationship(s) with you,*
> *I love you, honor you, and appreciate you.*

Please forgive my ancestors and me for all the mistakes we have made in all lifetimes that have hurt or harmed you or your ancestors in any way.
I am sincerely sorry for all these mistakes.
I forgive you and your ancestors totally, completely, and unconditionally for any and all hurt or harm you may have caused my ancestors or me in all lifetimes.
Thank you.

Say *hello* to outer souls:

Dear Tao Source and Divine,
Dear buddhas, saints (name the saints you believe in),
Dear Heaven, Mother Earth, and countless planets, stars, galaxies, and universes,
I love you, honor you, and appreciate you.
Please forgive my ancestors and me for all the mistakes, hurt, or harm we have caused in all lifetimes related to negative shen qi jing blockages created in all kinds of relationships.
I apologize from the bottom of my heart to you and to all the souls my ancestors and I have hurt or harmed in these ways.
In order to be forgiven, I will serve unconditionally.
To chant and meditate is to serve.
I will chant and meditate as much as I can.
I will offer unconditional service as much as I can.
I unconditionally forgive anyone who hurt or harmed me or my ancestors in all lifetimes.
I am extremely grateful.
Thank you.

Mind Power. Visualize golden light connecting you, your ancestors, and the people (or animals, organizations, cities, countries, etc.) from whom you have requested forgiveness.

Breath Power. Inhale and expand your abdomen. Exhale and contract your abdomen. Make sure you inhale and exhale smoothly, evenly, and naturally. Remember that the length of each inhalation and exhalation depends on your personal condition. Do not force anything. Nature's way is best.

Sound Power. As we chant, we combine the Sound Power with Breath Power and a more refined Mind Power visualization. See the video of this practice that includes my chanting.

Step 1

a. Inhale. Visualize golden light going from your nose down through the center of your body to the bottom of your torso, where it gathers as a ball in your first Soul House.

b. Exhale. Chant "Kuan Shu" (pronounced *kwahn shoo*). At the same time, visualize the golden light ball rotating up from the first Soul House to the Message Center (heart chakra), where it explodes and radiates in all directions.

c. Repeat steps 1a and 1b for a total of seven times.

Step 2

a. Inhale. Golden light goes from your nose down the central channel and gathers as a ball in your first Soul House.

b. Exhale. Chant "Kuan Shu Kuan Shu Kuan Shu." At the same time, visualize the golden light ball rotating up from the first Soul House to the Message Center, where it continues to rotate, explodes, and radiates in all directions.

c. Repeat steps 2a and 2b for a total of four times.

Step 3

a. Inhale. The golden light ball again gathers in your first Soul House.

b. Exhale. Chant:

   Kuan Shu (pronounced *kwahn shoo*)
   Kuan Shu Kuan Shu Kuan Shu
   Kuan Shu Kuan Shu Kuan Shu
   Kuan Shu Kuan Shu Kuan Shu
   Kuan Shu Kuan Shu Kuan Shu Kuan Shu

   As you chant these five lines, inhale quickly after each line and visualize the golden light ball rotating as follows:

When you chant line 1, the golden light ball rotates up from the first Soul House to the Message Center (fourth Soul House), and then down through the Kun Gong back to the first Soul House.

When you chant lines 2 through 5, the golden light ball rotates up from the first Soul House to the Message Center (heart chakra or fourth Soul House), and then down through the Kun Gong back to the first Soul House. Then, the golden ball makes a circle. It goes from the first Soul House into the spinal cord through an invisible hole in front of the tailbone, then flows up the spinal cord, into and through the brain up to the seventh Soul House atop your head. From there, it goes back down inside your nasal cavity to the palate, and then down through the fifth, fourth, third, and second Soul Houses back to the first Soul House.

c. Repeat steps 3a and 3b for a total of four times.

You may chant aloud or silently. Doing both yang and yin chanting every time you practice is best.

Tao Calligraphy Power. Trace *Da Kuan Shu,* greatest forgiveness. (See "How to find other Tao Calligraphies in order to apply Tao Calligraphy Power" on page 59 above.)

When you trace, tracing becomes your Body Power. You may combine tracing with Mind Power, Sound Power, and/or Breath Power if you wish, or you may simply focus on tracing.

Close. End your practice session by saying:

Hao. Hao. Hao.
Thank you. Thank you. Thank you.

ꕥ ꕥ ꕥ

This is how to apply six sacred Tao power techniques to heal and transform your relationships through Da Kuan Shu, greatest forgiveness.

You can practice for five to ten minutes. You can practice for a half-hour or an hour. There is no time limit. The more you practice, the more benefits you could receive.

Practice. Practice. Practice.

Experience the transformation.

12

Apply Six Sacred Tao Power Techniques to Heal and Transform Finances

THINK ABOUT THE ECONOMIC situation on Mother Earth at this time. Many people on Mother Earth are very wealthy. Many more people on Mother Earth are very poor.

Think about the people around you. Some people are very intelligent. You might think they should be very successful in business, but they may not be successful at all. Some people are very simple. They may even seem unintelligent, but they are very successful.

Why do some people have financial abundance? The root cause is positive shen qi jing. Such a person and his or her ancestors accumulated great virtue in their lifetimes. They served people very well in their lifetimes. For this good service, offered through love, care, compassion, sincerity, honesty, and more, they were given virtue.

This good virtue, which is recorded in the Akashic Records (see footnote 19 on page 89 for an explanation of the Akashic Records), has transformed to physical money in the person's current lifetime. If such a person continues to serve well, he or she will continue to have financial abundance in future lifetimes. Their descendants will also flourish.

Why do other people struggle with poor financial conditions? The root cause is negative shen qi jing. Such a person and his or her ancestors made significant mistakes in their lifetimes. The mistakes come through killing, cheating, stealing, taking advantage of others, and more.

Therefore, in order to transform finances, the key is to clear the negative shen qi jing blockages created and carried by you and your ancestors.

I would like to share the sacred wisdom and practice to transform your finances. A financial center within the body is the Lower Dan Tian. (See footnote 18 on page 89 for an explanation of the Lower Dan Tian and see figure 15 on page 90 for its location.)

We can heal and transform negative shen qi jing of finances in the Lower Dan Tian into positive shen qi jing by applying six sacred Tao power techniques.

Let us practice Da Chang Sheng, greatest flourishing, to heal and transform finances. I emphasize the power and significance of Da Chang Sheng.

The seventh of the Ten Da natures of Tao is greatest flourishing.
Tao Source bestows huge prosperity, luck, and success.
Offer kind service to accumulate virtue.
Tao career flourishes.

Body Power. Place your hands in the Yin Yang Palm position (figure 16) on the lower abdomen below the navel, over the Lower Dan Tian.

Soul Power. Say *hello* to inner souls:

> *Dear soul heart mind body of my finances,*
> *I love you, honor you, and appreciate you.*
> *Please forgive my ancestors and me for all the mistakes we have made in all lifetimes that have hurt or harmed anyone or anything financially or in business in any way.*
> *I deeply apologize for all of these mistakes.*
> *You also have the power to heal and transform yourselves.*

Please heal and transform (make a personal request for your finances or business).
Do a good job.
Thank you.

Say *hello* to outer souls:

Dear Tao Source and Divine,
Dear buddhas, saints (name the saints you believe in),
Dear Heaven, Mother Earth, and countless planets, stars, galaxies, and universes,
I love you, honor you, and appreciate you.
Please forgive my ancestors and me for all the mistakes, hurt, or harm we have caused in all lifetimes related to negative shen qi jing blockages in finances or in business.
I am sincerely sorry for all these mistakes.
I apologize from the bottom of my heart to you and to all the souls my ancestors and I have hurt or harmed in these ways.
In order to be forgiven, I will serve unconditionally.
To chant and meditate is to serve.
I will chant and meditate as much as I can.
I will offer unconditional service as much as I can.
I unconditionally forgive anyone who harmed the finances or businesses of me or my ancestors in all lifetimes.
I am extremely grateful.
Thank you.

Mind Power. Visualize golden light shining in and around the request you made for the transformation of your finances.

Breath Power. Inhale and expand your abdomen. Exhale and contract your abdomen. Make sure you inhale and exhale smoothly, evenly, and naturally. Remember that the length of each inhalation and exhalation depends on your personal condition. Follow nature's way.

Sound Power. As we chant, we combine the Sound Power with Breath Power and a more refined Mind Power visualization. See the video of this practice that includes my chanting.

Step 1

a. Inhale. Visualize golden light going from your nose down through the center of your body to the bottom of your torso, where it gathers as a ball in your first Soul House.

b. Exhale. Chant "Chang Sheng" (pronounced *chahng shung*). At the same time, visualize the golden light ball rotating up from the first Soul House to the Lower Dan Tian, where it explodes and radiates in all directions.

c. Repeat steps 1a and 1b for a total of seven times.

Step 2

a. Inhale. Golden light goes from your nose down the central channel and gathers as a ball in your first Soul House.

b. Exhale. Chant "Chang Sheng Chang Sheng Chang Sheng." At the same time, visualize the golden light ball rotating up from the first Soul House to the Lower Dan Tian, where it continues to rotate, explodes, and radiates in all directions.

c. Repeat steps 2a and 2b for a total of four times.

Step 3

a. Inhale. The golden light ball again gathers in your first Soul House.

b. Exhale. Chant:

   Chang Sheng (pronounced *chahng shung*)
   Chang Sheng Chang Sheng Chang Sheng
   Chang Sheng Chang Sheng Chang Sheng
   Chang Sheng Chang Sheng Chang Sheng
   Chang Sheng Chang Sheng Chang Sheng Chang Sheng

   As you chant these five lines, inhale quickly after each line and visualize the golden light ball rotating as follows:

   When you chant line 1, the golden light ball rotates up from the first Soul House to the Lower Dan Tian, up further to the Kun Gong, and then back down to the first Soul House.

When you chant lines 2 through 5, the golden light ball rotates up from the first Soul House to the Lower Dan Tian, up further to the Kun Gong, and then back down to the first Soul House. Then, the golden ball makes a circle. It goes from the first Soul House into the spinal cord through an invisible hole in front of the tailbone, then flows up the spinal cord, into and through the brain up to the seventh Soul House atop your head. From there, it goes back down inside your nasal cavity to the palate, and then down through the fifth, fourth, third, and second Soul Houses back to the first Soul House.

c. Repeat steps 3a and 3b for a total of four times.

You may chant aloud or silently. Doing both yang and yin chanting every time you practice is best.

Tao Calligraphy Power. Trace *Da Ai,* greatest love, or *Da Kuan Shu,* greatest forgiveness. (See "How to find other Tao Calligraphies in order to apply Tao Calligraphy Power" on page 59 above.)

When you trace, tracing becomes your Body Power. You may combine tracing with Mind Power, Sound Power, and/or Breath Power if you wish, or you may simply focus on tracing.

Close. End your practice session by saying:

Hao. Hao. Hao.
Thank you. Thank you. Thank you.

ꕥ ꕥ ꕥ

This is how to apply the six sacred Tao power techniques to heal and transform your finances through Da Chang Sheng, greatest flourishing. You can practice for five to ten minutes. You can practice for a half-hour or an hour. There is no time limit. The more you practice, the more benefits you could receive.

Da Chang Sheng is the seventh of the Ten Da natures of Tao. You can apply any of the other nine Da qualities in the same way for transforming your finances.

Practice. Practice. Practice.

Experience the transformation.

Conclusion

EVERYONE AND EVERYTHING IN countless planets, stars, galaxies, and universes, including human beings, are made of shen qi jing. Shen includes soul, heart, and mind. In quantum science and Tao Science, soul is information or message. The spiritual heart is the receiver of the message. Mind is the processor of the message. Qi, energy, is the mover of the message. Jing, matter, is the transformer of the message.

Shen qi jing form an information or message system for a being. Soul leads the heart. Heart leads the mind. Mind moves the energy. Energy moves the matter.

Why does a person have good health, good relationships, and good finances? It is due to positive shen qi jing.

Why does a person have health, relationship, or financial challenges, as well as other challenges in life? It is due to negative shen qi jing.

This book shares six sacred Tao power techniques: Body Power, Sound Power, Mind Power, Soul Power, Breath Power, and Tao Calligraphy Power. These techniques connect with Heaven, Mother Earth, and countless planets, stars, galaxies, and universes, as well as with saints within all realms, to bring positive Tao Source, Heaven, and Mother Earth shen qi jing to you to empower you to transform your negative shen qi jing in health, relationships, finances, and every aspect of life.

There is an important ancient wisdom: *da Dao zhi jian* 大道至簡. "Da" means *greatest*. "Dao" is *Tao Source*. "Zhi" means *extremely*. "Jian" means *simple*. "Da Dao zhi jian" means *the greatest Tao is extremely simple*.

Each practice in this book, whether to heal your five elements, to heal your mental and spiritual bodies, to heal your Soul Houses and Wai Jiao, to heal your Shen Qi Jing Channels, to heal your relationships, or to heal your finances, is very simple. It could be hard for some people to believe. Practice along with my chanting in the videos that have been created for you. Know that we have collected good research results where people have received remarkable healing and transformation from similar techniques and practices. We have hundreds of heart-touching and moving results people have achieved by practicing these techniques. I have gathered some of these cases from our research studies in an appendix that follows.

In ancient wisdom, *if you want to know if a pear is sweet, taste it*. The current wisdom is *if you want to know if anything works, experience it*.

I have shared with humanity repeatedly for the last seven years that connecting with the Tao Calligraphy healing field using sacred Tao techniques is the simplest way to heal and transform. I always say:

Experience the transformation.

I wish for each reader to practice with these techniques to transform your health, relationships, and finances and uplift your spiritual journey.

Practice. Practice. Practice.

Experience the transformation.

I love my heart and soul
I love all humanity
Join hearts and souls together
Love, peace, and harmony
Love, peace, and harmony

Appendix

Tao Calligraphy Healing Field Research Case Studies

by Peter Hudoba, MD, FRCS

RESEARCH INTO THE EFFECTS of Tao Calligraphy healing field practice and Tao Calligraphy Light Field transmissions has been ongoing across several different studies for the last several years. I would like to share some representative interim results from a recent study-in-progress sponsored by Sha Research Foundation, based in San Francisco, California, of which I am the research director.

The study was designed as a prospective follow-up study focusing on Tao Calligraphy movement meditation, which you have learned from this book is Tao Calligraphy Power through Dan (lower abdomen) tracing, with mantra chanting (Sound Power). The Institutional Review Board (IRB) in Aurora, Ontario, Canada approved the study in 2017 and the study commenced in January 2018.

Study subjects came from the United States and Canada. They suffered from various medically diagnosed physical or emotional conditions. All subjects received a personal healing blessing and one or more Tao Calligraphy Light Field transmissions from Dr. and Master Zhi Gang Sha. They were instructed to practice daily for one to two hours using Sound Power and Tao Calligraphy Power, and also incorporating Soul Power, Body Power, and Mind Power. In addition, thirty-minute group practice sessions led by trained instructors were offered twice a week. Participation was strongly encouraged but voluntary.

The self-practice instructions were as follows:

- **Body Power.** Stand or sit comfortably.
- **Mind Power.** Visualize golden light in and around the unhealthy area or, for emotional conditions, the related organ.
- **Sound Power.** Chant appropriate mantras.
- **Soul Power.** Say *hello* to request light and love for healing from inner souls and outer souls.
- **Tao Calligraphy Power.** Stand and do Dan tracing as much as possible. Otherwise, sit and trace with five fingertips.

Subjects were encouraged to continue any treatment they were engaged in with conventional or complementary/alternative healthcare practitioners. No medical diagnosis or advice was given to subjects.

Most of the results shared in this appendix are from the first quarter of 2019, essentially an interim follow up after one year. More recent information is available for some subjects as indicated in the detail. The study is continuing into and will end in 2020.

Case 1

- Female on disability for stage four endometriosis diagnosed in March 2011 with extensive pelvic adhesions.
- Suffered tremendous pain in abdomen for many years, with very heavy menses. Could not function. Become depressed, anxious, and suicidal.
- Unable to have bowel movements due to adhesions in sigmoid from endometriosis, and had been giving herself an enema almost every day.
- Treated with Lupron, hormone replacement therapy, and contraceptives.
- An MRI in February 2014 revealed large ovarian cysts, uterine adenomyosis, and adhesions constricting the colon.
- She planned a hysterectomy and removal of ovaries.

- In April 2014 she received a healing blessing from Dr. and Master Sha for her endometriosis. Almost immediately after the healing blessing, she experienced total peace and her suicidal thoughts stopped. Moreover, her pain level was reduced by ninety percent (her personal evaluation). The pain level increased later to some degree, but never to the prior levels.
- In July 2014 she had a follow up consultation with a surgeon, who said that based on the latest tests, a hysterectomy and removal of ovaries were not needed.
- Also, because of some previous adverse reactions to her medications (Lupron, hormone replacement therapy, contraceptives), the surgeon recommended no medication and that further tests would be done only if any symptoms returned.
- She started to work with a nutritionist and to use a progesterone cream to help with remaining symptoms of endometriosis.
- Has practiced tracing of the "Da Ai" Tao Calligraphy card daily as much as she was able and often practiced along with videos of Dr. and Master Sha tracing in the Tao Calligraphy healing field.
- In January 2018 she received another healing blessing from Dr. and Master Sha. Her symptoms continued to improve markedly.
- She received numerous Tao Calligraphy Light Field transmissions throughout 2019.
- Her menses have become less heavy and the associated pain is mostly gone.
- She started losing excess weight.
- Her constipation (due to constriction in sigmoid) that required a daily enema has improved by eighty percent.
- She no longer feels the sharp pain in the colon that she previously experienced during all of her periods.
- Gradually, pain in her knees and lower back has improved and significant swelling in her ankles has completely resolved.
- In 2019, after years of disability, she returned to work as a part-time office assistant for the school board and later moved to a full-time job at another office, with a daily commute of two hours.
- She was also able to travel abroad for the first time in years.

- Blood work in January 2019 showed that almost all values were within the normal range.
- X-rays in December 2018 found only "minimal evidence of osteoarthritis."
- An ultrasound administered in December 2018 noted:
  - Adenomyosis and uterine fibroids stable since 2014
  - Bilateral ovarian endometriosis decreased from 2014

Case 2

- Female diagnosed in 2007 with chronic lymphocytic leukemia and autoimmune hemolytic anemia.
- Received first personal healing blessings from Dr. and Master Sha in 2013.
- Immediately afterward in 2013, she began sporadic practices of meditation and qigong. Her condition was stable, with no deterioration.
- In April 2015 she became very weak after walking five blocks to a bank, so she continued walking to the nearest hospital emergency room with shortness of breath.
- She was immediately admitted to ICU with HB 22 g/L and WBC 1070.
- A CT scan showed an enlarged spleen, enlarged lymph nodes, and a tumor on the liver.
- She was treated in the ICU for one week with chemotherapy, Prednisone, and transfusions. After discharge, she took only Prednisone for five months.
- When she left the ICU in May 2015, she started to receive Tao Calligraphy distance healing daily for three months.
- She started to practice with Tao Calligraphy daily as well as practicing other meditations and qigong daily.
- In September 2015 (five months after admission to the ICU), she consulted a specialist again. Her WBC dropped from 1070 to 99.
- She stopped taking Prednisone and receiving transfusions (for anemia).

- In May 2016 she was evaluated by a specialist again: WBC 103, HB 117 g/L. Note that she achieved these improved results without chemotherapy or transfusions.

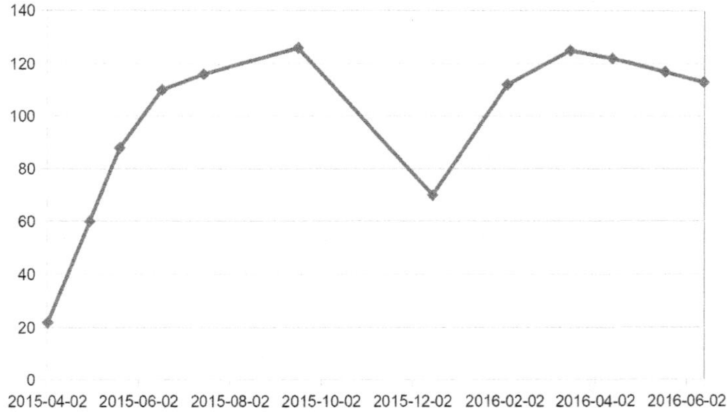

Red Blood Cell Count

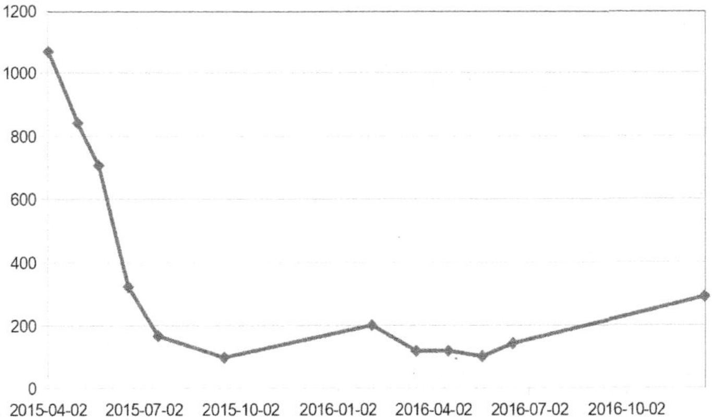

White Blood Cell Count

- In March 2017 (nearly two years after admission to ICU), she remains in good health, is positive and at peace with her illness, feels balanced emotionally, feels good energy and stamina, and can perform all normal activities of daily life.
- She is planning to start a business.

Case 3

- Female. When she was five years old, her mother nearly died. The subject developed intense social anxiety, physical pain (nerve spasms in intestines), intense anger, and feelings of disconnection and detachment. These worsened when her father began to drink heavily.
- As an adult she has suffered from night terrors every day, waking up completely shaken and terrified with heart racing, heavy breathing, and completely soaked with cold sweat.
- She also suffered from pervasive grief from her childhood trauma.
- She has been doing foundational practices daily with forgiveness, chanting, and Tao Calligraphy Power together for about one-and-a-half hours.
- In January 2018 she received Tao Calligraphy healing field blessings and permanent light field transmissions from Dr. and Master Sha. The next night, she was able to sleep through the night without any night terrors. She said, "The sleep was truly peaceful."
- She has since received several additional Tao Calligraphy Light Field transmissions for her condition.
- As of November 2019, she is able to go to sleep without worry and experiences no nightmares. She awakens fresh and rested.
- Symptoms of fright/terror, racing heart, sweating, and waking from nightmares have completely resolved.
- She is no longer afraid, apprehensive, or reluctant to go to sleep.
- She feels joy and happiness, which she considers incredible.

Case 4

- This 78-year-old female suffers from a genetic disorder: abundant colon.
- Her large intestine coils around itself in the right and left quadrants with partial bowel obstruction.
- She suffered from mild constipation throughout life.
- In 2015 she contracted amoebic dysentery in a foreign country.
- Since then she has experienced severe abdominal pains, significant weight loss, major constipation, and abdominal bloating.

- Medications include hyoscyamine and Linzess.
- Enrolled into the study and received initial healing blessings and Tao Calligraphy Light Field transmissions in January 2018.
- Received further light field transmissions and healing blessings in September 2019 for various organs, organ systems, and energy centers.
- Practices about two hours a day.
- Constipation is completely gone for the first time in her life.
- The partial bowel obstruction is completely gone.
- Sensation of abdominal bloating is more than ninety percent relieved.
- Pain is greatly reduced.
- Feels more peaceful, grateful, and tolerant.
- Able to take care of her property, rentals, and garden completely, and even helps her elderly tenants and her disabled sister.

Case 5

- In 2013 this now thirty-five-year-old female suffered from progressively worsening headaches and began to lose hearing in her right ear.
- Examination revealed no neurological deficit besides the hearing loss.
- In 2013 she was diagnosed from an MRI with vestibular schwannoma, 20 x 21 mm.
- In 2014 the tumor grew to 27 mm and she had surgery to remove it.
- The surgeon left a residue of 5 mm on the facial nerve to preserve the nerve.
- An MRI in 2017 showed that this residue grew to 10 mm.
- She was offered a gamma knife radiosurgical procedure but she decided not to proceed.
- Medications include painkillers and dexamethasone.
- Saw several energy healers.
- After meeting Dr. and Master Sha, she began practicing with Tao Calligraphy, forgiveness, and chanting, anywhere from thirty minutes to six hours a day.

- In September 2019 she had a personal consultation with Dr. and Master Sha and received clearing of some negative shen qi jing blockages.
- She also received two permanent light field transmissions for her condition, as well as light field transmissions for brain, heart, liver, kidneys, ear nerves, central nervous system, immune system, endocrine system, digestive system, and lymphatic system.
- Waiting for results of October 2019 MRI.
- Feels more sensitive and feels stronger energies and vibrations in the body.
- Feels really light; tightness in the head has relaxed.

Case 6

- This sixty-six-year-old female has suffered from outbursts of anger, nausea, and vomiting every morning, stiffness in the left knee, cataracts for thirteen years, and pain from a torn right biceps ligament for three years.
- Upon entering the study in January 2018, she received healing blessings and a light transmission for healing anger.
- She practices with Tao Calligraphy Power and Sound Power (chanting).
- In July 2019 she reported:
  - Cataracts improved for six months after the healing blessings, but more recently became worse.
  - Discomfort from the torn biceps ligament has reduced.
  - Anger outbursts have improved by twenty to thirty percent in frequency and severity.
  - Morning nausea and vomiting are completely gone.

Case 7

- Female, age 55.
- Diagnosed in 2017 with burnout from excessive stress (long work hours and demanding care for family members).
- Suffered from poor memory and difficulty focusing.

- In stressful situations, she would stutter and could no longer speak normally.
- Developed insomnia.
- Many tasks and activities took longer than normal to accomplish.
- Developed high blood pressure in stressful occasions and would become dizzy.
- Prescribed Candecor comp. and escitalopram (for depression) and lercanidipine (for high blood pressure).
- Was released from work in 2017.
- Daily practices include Tao Calligraphy tracing and chanting; also attends Tao Calligraphy healing field group practice sessions.
- Received healing blessings and permanent light field transmissions upon enrolling in the study in January 2018.
- Her ability to focus has improved.
- Stuttering improved significantly; now speaks normally.
- One year later (early 2019), her depressive symptoms improved to the point where she was able to stop her medications for depression.
- One-and-a-half years later (late Spring 2019), she stopped her high blood pressure medication.
- She is still on sick leave from work with burnout.

Case 8

- This fifty-seven-year-old female has suffered from agoraphobia with panic attacks for forty-three years, since she was fourteen.
- Agoraphobia is anxiety in situations where the person perceives their environment to be unsafe with no easy way to escape. These environments can include open spaces, public transit, shopping centers, or simply being outside their home.
- Her emotional pain has usually been at level eight on a scale from zero (no pain) to ten (highest, excruciating pain).
- Anxiety impacts her ability to function and is strongest with other people when she is outside. She cannot drive a car for example.
- She has consulted naturopaths, psychologists, herbalists, acupuncturists, cognitive behavioral therapists, and other healers

and taken vitamin supplements in an unfruitful search for a solution.

- Upon joining the study and subsequently, she has received several clearings of negative shen qi jing blockages and numerous Tao Calligraphy Light Field transmissions.
- She has done her self-healing practices, including forgiveness, Tao Calligraphy tracing, and chanting, for one-and-one-half hours daily.
- As of November 2019, she:
  - feels better overall
  - finds it much easier to be among and with people, with little or no anxiety
  - is more stable emotionally, in particular has less anger
  - is actually able to relax
  - is more aware of her behavior and is consciously trying to improve

Case 9

- This seventy-year-old female has suffered from arthritis with inflammation throughout her entire body. Her musculoskeletal issues involve the neck, spine, shoulders, hips, knees, hands, and all joints.
- Arthritis started forty-five years ago in her knees.
- Her wrists become painfully inflamed. The inflammation and pain were at times so intense that she could not take care of herself, walk normally, or carry or hold even the lightest of objects.
- When her whole body was inflamed, she could not leave her home.
- Hip pain arose because her hips became misaligned from inflammation. In turn, her muscles were strained trying to compensate for the imbalances in her stance and stride, resulting in chronic and at times spastic muscle pain.
- Medications include anti-inflammatories and Plaquenil 200 mg. daily.
- She has also sought relief from traditional Chinese medicine, herbology, acupuncture, and herbal teas.

- Since being introduced to Dr. and Master Sha's soul healing system in 2010, she has received clearings of negative shen qi jing blockages and various light field transmissions.
- In 2010 she received a healing blessing from Dr. and Master Sha for her swollen knees. The swelling disappeared almost instantly and has not returned.
- She practices forgiveness, Tao Calligraphy tracing, and chanting.
- In December 2018 her rheumatologist was so pleased with her improvement that he reduced the dosage of Plaquenil from 200 mg. to 100 mg. daily.
- A recent x-ray (January 2020) reported degenerative changes of the hands and feet. There was no radiographic evidence of an inflammatory arthropathy.
- She is now able to move fully, including using her hands fully and turning her neck, which at times before felt fused.
- She is now free of hip and muscle pain, and no longer needs a cane to walk.

Case 10

- This fifty-year-old male was diagnosed in 1984 with "gay lymph node syndrome" and presumed acute onset of HIV infection.
- In 1986 he was confirmed to be HIV positive.
- In the early 1990s he received a diagnosis of AIDS, based on a declining T-cell count below 200.
- In 1990 he started monotherapy.
- In 1996 he was hospitalized with AIDS-related pneumonia and a T-cell count of 7.
- In 1997 he started combination antiretroviral therapy.
- After 1997 his T-cell count slowly climbed back to the mid-500 range and his health stabilized.
- In 2006 he met Dr. and Master Sha and began using Soul Power and receiving healing field blessings,
- He has continued with combination antiretroviral therapy but also received numerous light field transmissions.
- He practices self-healing meditations and Tao Calligraphy tracing daily.

- In 2013 his T-cell count returned to the fully normal range (over 700), where it has remained.
- He enjoys continued stable health and leads a fully active life, including full-time work.

so so cs

The overall conclusions of this entire research study, from which we have provided the above sampling of cases, can be summarized as follows:

- Meditation with tracing Tao Calligraphy and including Body Power, Soul Power, Mind Power, and Sound Power was easy to learn, well tolerated, and no complications arose.

- The results of this study confirmed the efficacy of combining light field transmissions of positive information and energies and Tao Calligraphy tracing with conventional medical treatment.

About the Author

DR. AND MASTER ZHI Gang Sha is a world-renowned healer, transformational leader, Tao Grandmaster, philanthropist, worldwide humanitarian, and creator of Tao Calligraphy healing fields and thousands of healers and teachers. He is the founder of and author of books on Soul Mind Body Medicine™, a complete soul healing system, and Tao Science, the science of creation and grand unification. Dr. and Master Sha has written twenty-six books in English, including eleven *New York Times* bestsellers, a Soul Power Series, and a Heart and Soul Series.

An M.D. in China and a doctor of traditional Chinese medicine in China and Canada, Dr. and Master Sha is the founder of Tao Academy™ and Love Peace Harmony Foundation™, which is dedicated to helping families worldwide create happier and healthier lives. A grandmaster of many ancient disciplines, including tai chi, qigong, kung fu, *I Ching*, and feng shui, Dr. and Master Sha was named Qigong Master of the Year at the Fifth World Congress on Qigong.

In 2006 Dr. and Master Sha was honored with the prestigious Martin Luther King, Jr. Commemorative Commission Award for his humanitarian efforts. In 2016 he received rare and prestigious appointments as Shu Fa Jia (書法家 National Chinese Calligrapher Master) and Yan Jiu Yuan (研究員 Honorable Researcher Professor), the highest titles a Chinese calligrapher can receive, by the State Ethnic of Academy of Painting in China.

Printed in Great Britain
by Amazon

19117280R00108